It's Just a Phase:

The Anxious Goddess' Tools for Making Mental Health Magic

Jamie Hanley

Illustrated by Kelly Rose Burgess

IT'S JUST A PHASE by Jamie Hanley
Published by IG Introspections, an imprint of Inspired Girl Publishing Group, a division of Inspired Girl Enterprises
inspiredgirlbooks.com

Inspired Girl Publishing Group is honored to bring forth books with heart and stories that matter. We are proud to offer this book to our readers; the techniques, the methods, and the words are the author's alone.

This book is written as a source of information only. The information contained in this book should by no means be considered a substitute for the advice of a qualified medical professional. In addition, the publisher and the author assume no responsibility for errors, inaccuracies, omissions, or any other inconsistencies herein. The use of this book implies your acceptance of this disclaimer.

Products, books, trademarks, and trademark names are used throughout this book to describe and inform the reader about various proprietary products that are owned by third parties. No endorsement of the information contained in this book is given by the owners of such products and trademarks, and no endorsement is implied by the inclusion of products, books, or trademarks in this book.

© 2024 Jamie Hanley

All rights reserved. No portion of this book may be reproduced in any form without permission from the publisher, except as permitted by U.S. copyright law. For permissions: help@inspiredgirlbooks.com

ISBN: 979-8-9897899-4-8
Written by: Jamie Hanley
Editorial Director: Jenn Tuma-Young
Copy Editor: Natalie Papailiou
Front Cover Design: Kelly Rose Burgess
Book Design and Typeset: Kelly Rose Burgess
Author Photo by: Claire Sheprow, Find Orion Photography

Library of Congress Control Number: 2024932955

To Jemma and Ronan,
may you embrace all the qualities
that make you one of a kind. I love
you to the Moon and back.

Hello Lovely Human,

Have you ever noticed someone who appears to stay calm, cool, and collected, and wished that you could find that vibe? There's a secret to their inner peace - it requires a lot of tools, internal work, messiness, healing, and commitment.

Sometimes merely existing in this intense world feels like A LOT. We all experience mental health challenges and difficult emotions — it's part of being human.

If you've picked up this book, you already know it's possible to feel lighter and less overwhelmed, you just need the tools. Whether you're in a challenging season or a stressful situation, having coping skills in your corner will bolster you to not only survive, but thrive.

Within these pages you'll find a wellness apothecary. Connecting with spirituality and nature, paying attention to cycles, and harnessing the knowledge of your most powerful internal and external resources is the recipe for making mental health magic.

The inspiration for creating this book was both personal and professional. The practices herein are tried and true interventions I've used to regulate my own nervous system and taught to hundreds of clients. Art and creativity have always been integral in my life. After the birth of my son, I experienced postpartum anxiety. Art therapy, crafting, and mindful coloring became an essential part of recovery. As a therapist leading groups throughout my career, old-school worksheets felt lackluster, so I sought a creative spin to make learning about mental health more engaging.

The call to pull this knowledge together started during the pandemic. I was grateful to have a variety of evidence-based coping skills while parenting, schooling, and working as a mental health counselor. My toolbox was full of cognitive behavioral therapy, dialectical behavior therapy, and yoga techniques for dealing with anxiety. Attuning to nature's seasons and the moon's phases provided a sense of time and connection. When everything felt uncertain, the Moon - the same moon our ancestors gazed at - provided assurance that we all go through phases, each of them temporary. This is my recipe for mental health magic. May you find the insights and practices herein equally beneficial in your healing process.

Welcome to a world where emotions are your superpower. You belong here.

xxoo
Jamie

Table of Contents

Introduction - Change is the only Constant   1

Part 1 - The Study of Cycles   4

Part 2 - Resources by the light of the Moon   55

New Moon - Set the Foundation of Caring and Tending to Yourself   56

Waxing Crescent - Contemplating Change   70

First Quarter - Identify and Add External Resources   80

Waxing Gibbous - Add and Strengthen Internal Resources   88

Full Moon - Time to shine   104

Waning Gibbous - Authentic Communication and Assertiveness   108

Third Quarter - Make time for Rest & Reflection   114

Waning Crescent - Embracing the Shadow   120

Super Moon - Super Charged Spiritual Practices   126

Part 3 - Coloring Pages and Creative Prompts   140

Introduction - Change is the Only Constant

Our lives are experienced in cycles. Whether from birth until death, the seasons throughout each year, the moon each month, the cycle of the nervous system, women's menstrual cycle, or the twenty-four hours in a day, our lives are lived in patterns.

Change happens in cyclical patterns and upward spirals. Every year, as we revolve around the Sun, we learn, grow, and evolve if we choose. As humans we will experience highs and lows of life, trauma and ecstasy, grief and joy. The emotional rollercoaster of our lived experience is real.

In order to navigate the nonlinear nature of life, we need an arsenal of mental health skills, which may include education, psychotherapy, group therapy, creative outlets, exercise, relaxation, meditation, medication and ANY other practices that help our nervous system stay calm and connected. These are called resources and this book is full of them.

Resources are the supports and strategies to keep at the top of our minds to care for our mental health and build overall resilience.

How to Use this Book

This workbook is structured to experiment and see what helps calm your mind and relax your nervous system. It's important to engage with the activities in the book - some resources will work like magic, and others might not. It's important to try things a few times; you may notice different situations call for different skills. In any kind of creative endeavor or mindfulness practice, we must take the time to dedicate and practice over and over and over to improve. Insight arrives when we notice how past experiences keep us stuck in unhealthy emotional patterns and fighting the natural flow of cycles and change adds to stress and overwhelm.

Keeping track of how you feel as you move through these cycles and seasons is valuable insight as you become a diligent student of your personal mental health and wellness needs.

One of the greatest gifts of our lifetime is to be a student of ourselves.

There's quizzes, journal prompts, and insightful inquiries to help you research yourself. Make notes in the book, dog ear the pages - use this workbook to study yourself!

Get ready to tap into the magic of cycles and useful resources for ongoing emotional healing and wellbeing.

Part 1
The Study of Cycles

The first steps on this healing journey invite a deeper look into the cyclical nature of being human, and what that looks like for you. No two people are alike, which means

YOU are the FOREMOST EXPERT on YOURSELF!

You'll study your own cycles, patterns, and habits to figure out what you'd like to change.

The Cycle of Change

We've all heard it before, "people only change when they want to change." Change is challenging and often uncomfortable. Staying the same can be uncomfortable too. We often develop patterns of dealing with those uncomfortable feelings in ways that feel helpful in the short term, but aren't the best choices in the long run. Only when an individual is ready to change their behaviors will they choose to do so.

Healing is a lifelong process. Negative thoughts, feelings, and behaviors resurface in difficult times. It's easy to slip into old patterns of unhelpful behaviors. What matters is how many times we get back up and begin again. This is the Upward Cycle of Change (Prochaska and DiClementi, 1983). There are several phases in the cycle of change, strikingly similar to the moon's phases.

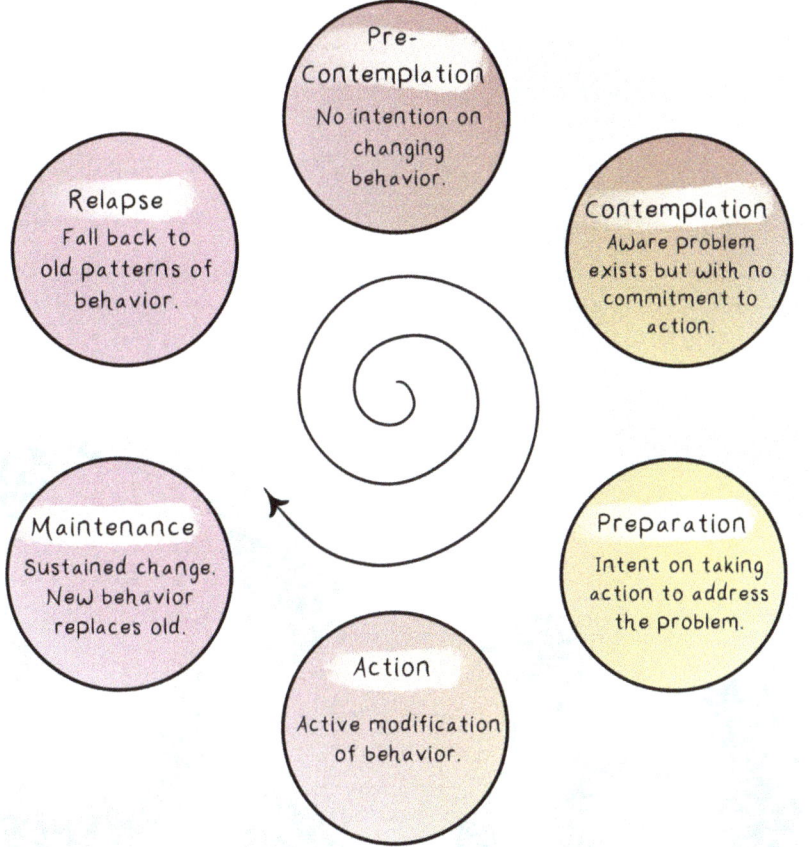

Every time we move through the cycle of change, we evolve. All cycles follow a similar pattern of birth, growth, peak, decline, and death. As the cycle is completed, we are able to let go and release, to create space for the next revolution. When we intensify our awareness of these cycles and how each phase impacts our mental health and wellness, we can harness the magic of alignment with a universal energy that works in our favor.

In this way, no effort is ever wasted. If you experience a lapse or relapse in your mental health and wellbeing, it doesn't mean you start over at the beginning or lose the knowledge you've gained. It means you need to revisit what works for you and refresh your plan.

If you are a person who feels connected to cycles in any way, harnessing the greater energy of mother nature that infinitely surrounds us can greatly help you find the harmony and balance you're seeking. When we align with and honor the energy of each phase, we are able to better manage expectations of ourselves and others during those times.

Activity Cycle of Change Worksheet

Bring to mind a situation or habit you want to change. Explore each phase of implementing change using the journaling questions below.

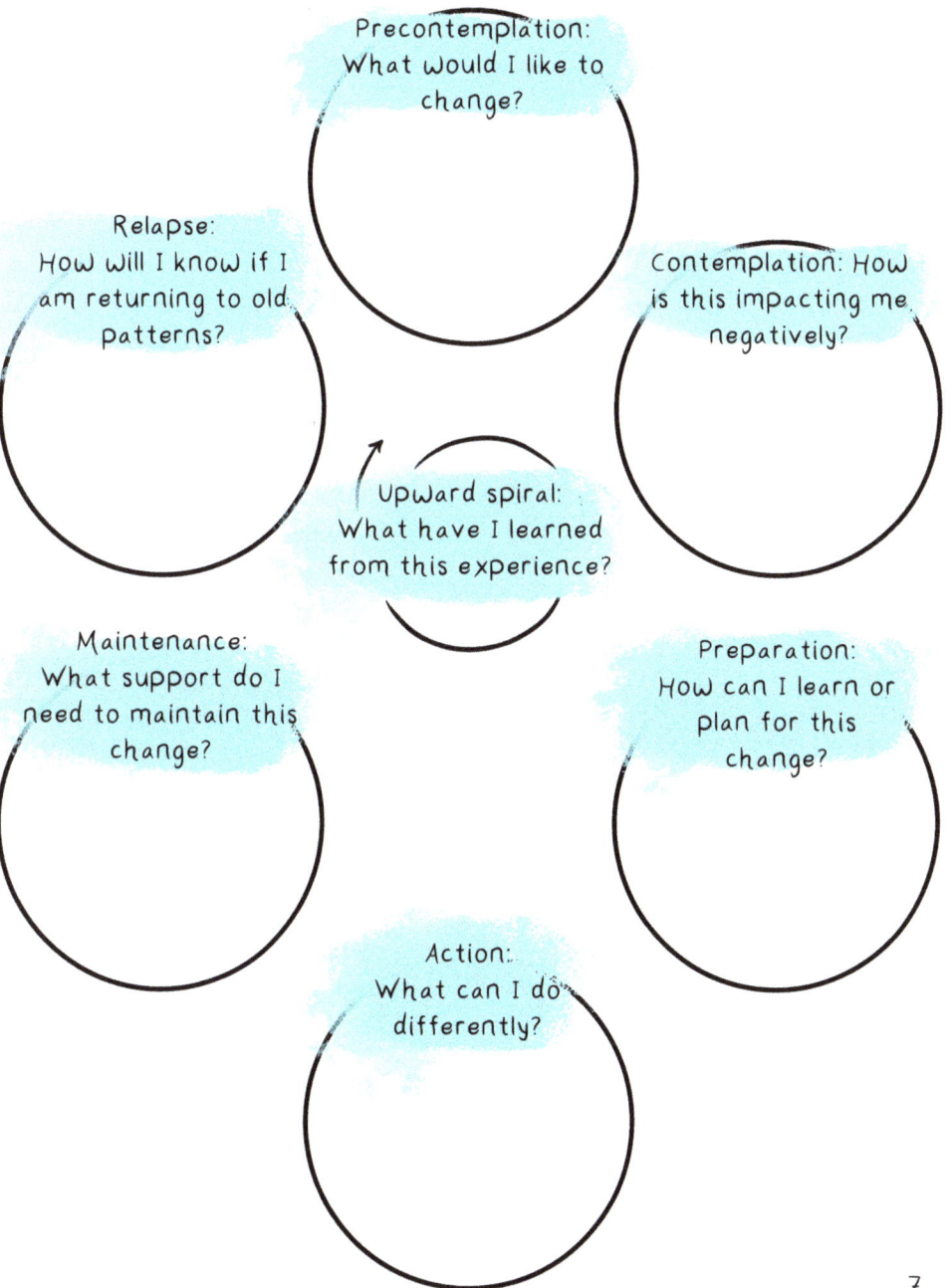

Daily Cycles

Notice how you feel throughout the day to bring insight to times when you can support yourself more, in order to align your energy and efforts for maximum impact and quality rest.

Ask yourself the following:

How do I feel upon waking?

When do I feel the most energized?

When do I feel the most sluggish?

How does the time of day impact my mood and energy levels?

What else do you notice about your energy throughout the day?

Quiz — Are you an early bird or a night owl?

Remember that there are no right or wrong answers.
All that matters is what's true for you.

I am most productive in the
- a) Morning
- b) Midday
- c) Afternoon
- d) Evening

I prefer to exercise in the
- a) Morning
- b) Midday
- c) Afternoon
- d) Evening

My mood is most positive in the
- a) Morning
- b) Midday
- c) Afternoon
- d) Evening

I like to socialize in the
- a) Morning
- b) Midday
- c) Afternoon
- d) Evening

I am able to concentrate best in the
- a) Morning
- b) Midday
- c) Afternoon
- d) Evening

My mood and energy tend to be lower in the
- a) Evening
- b) Afternoon
- c) Midday
- d) Morning

If you answered mostly a's and b's you're an early bird.
If you answered mostly c's and d's you're a night owl.

Examples of a Daily Routine

Early Bird

Sunrise - a magical, in-between time, early morning can be lovely time to meditate or practice morning rituals. How would you like to start your day?
- Wake at 5:30am
- Exercise
- Shower
- Pack lunches

Mid-morning - if your energy increases, this can be an ideal time for exercise, reflection, and getting yourself set up for a positive day. What are the essential parts of your morning routine?
- Breakfast and coffee
- Centering
- Tidy my space
- Journal
- Clear inbox

Noon - the most energizing part of the day for many, this is a good time to kick productivity into high gear or get out into the world. How can you maximize this time?
- Connect with friends and colleagues
- Post on social media
- Eat lunch

Mid-afternoon - this is often a time when people get tired, reaching for coffee or sugar to push through. What activities help you overcome this slump?
- Have a snack
- Get outside
- Movement
- Creativity

Sunset - the other in-between time of day, sunset is an ideal time for winding down. What are your favorite ways to spend the evening hours?
- Eat dinner
- Build a fire
- Tidy up and prepare for next day

Night - what rituals and routine can you create for a restful night's sleep? Notice the best time for you to go to bed and the optimal amount of sleep you need to support your mood and energy.
- Take a bath
- Read
- Listen to relaxing music
- Gentle movement

Fill in your own routine

Early Bird

Sunrise -

Mid-morning -

Noon -

Mid-afternoon -

Sunset -

Night -

Examples of a Daily Routine

Night Owl

Sunrise - a magical, in-between time, early morning can be lovely time to meditate or practice morning rituals. How would you like to start your day?
- Rest
- Start the day slowly

Mid-morning - if your energy increases, this can be an ideal time for exercise, reflection, and getting yourself set up for a positive day. What are the essential parts of your morning routine?
- Breakfast and coffee
- Exercise
- Journal

Noon - the most energizing part of the day for many, this is a good time to kick productivity into high gear or get out into the world. How can you maximize this time?
- Run errands
- Eat lunch
- Clear inbox

Mid-afternoon - this is often a time when people get tired, reaching for coffee or sugar to push through. What activities help you overcome this slump?
- Have a snack
- Get outside
- Movement

Sunset - the other in-between time of day, sunset is an ideal time for winding down. What are your favorite ways to spend the evening hours?
- Eat dinner
- Socialize
- Reach out to friends

Night - what rituals and routine can you create for a restful night's sleep? Notice the best time for you to go to bed and the optimal amount of sleep you need to support your mood and energy.
- Shower
- Creative practices
- Reading
- Journaling
- Sleep meditation

Fill in your own routine

Night Owl

Sunrise -

Mid-morning -

Noon -

Mid-afternoon -

Sunset -

Night -

Tap into the times you have more energy and positive moods and consider how you want to use it. This may be the best time to tackle a big project, work out, be social, experience intimacy, or do anything that you know requires more of your mental or physical energy reserves. When you know you feel lethargic, support your body's need to rest, relax, and refill your tank.

Take any opportunity possible to practice routines and rituals and tap into your resources.

How does your daily routine vibe with nature and your environment?

Having this macro-level awareness can help you align with Mother Nature and how she supports our energy levels. This will depend on where you live, your climate, and the time of year. It is unique to you. The practice of aligning your day with activities that support the needs of your mind, body, and spirit will also help heal the circadian rhythm, which helps our bodies rest.

Circadian Rhythm: Sleep and Wake Cycles

Sleep has an enormous impact on our emotions. Regardless of our age, if our sleep and wake cycles are off, we are likely to be cranky. In a 24-hour day, we have the opportunity to exist in both darkness and light, depending on the season and our location on the planet. When we don't experience enough light during the day, or when we spend too much time in front of screens at night, we are interfering with these cycles.

If you think your sleep cycles are off and it may be impacting your mood, it may be time for sleep hygiene - cleaning up your bedtime routine.

Brush up on beauty sleep by getting more natural light during the day, setting regular sleep and wake times, and turning off screens an hour before bed. Blackout curtains if you live in a city, a sleep mask, and a satin pillowcase can also set the stage for sleep.

Adults should aim for seven to nine hours of sleep. Notice what time you're getting to bed and when you are waking, as well as if you wake during the night.

My Sleep Story

I fall asleep at ____ pm

and wake at ____ am

which equals ____ hours

of sleep.

I wake up ____ times throughout the night.

When I wake at night

I (do/don't) fall back asleep easily.

I (do/don't) feel rested upon waking.

Many people find a bedtime routine helpful to fall asleep.

Bedtime Routine Suggestions

- Wash up, spray bedtime lavender fragrance, read
- Bathe, relaxing music, legs up the wall restorative yoga pose
- Shower, read, sleep meditation

Others may need help getting back to sleep in the middle of the night. Avoid the temptation to look at your phone or other screens if you wake in the middle of the night. Try counting backwards from one hundred and breathing deeply. If you are wide awake, try changing your location and reading a book until you are tired again, so as not to lay in bed ruminating about sleep.

Activity

Hone in on the daily routines that suit you best based on whether you are an early bird, a night owl, or in-between. Use this space to plan what helps you set yourself up for success on a daily basis and wind down to rest. These routines create structure, which helps us feel a sense of control and quells anxiety.

Reflection

Sunrise -

A magical, in-between time, early morning can be lovely time to meditate or practice morning rituals. How would you like to start your day?

Mid-morning -

If your energy increases, this can be an ideal time for exercise, reflection, and getting yourself set up for a positive day. What are the essential parts of your morning routine?

Noon -

The most energizing part of the day for many, this is a good time to kick productivity into high gear or get out into the world. How can you maximize this time?

Mid-afternoon -

This is often a time when people get tired, reaching for coffee or sugar to push through. What activities help you overcome this slump?

Sunset -

The other in-between time of day, sunset is an ideal time for winding down. What are your favorite ways to spend the evening hours?

Night -

What rituals and routine can you create for a restful night's sleep? Notice the best time for you to go to bed and the optimal amount of sleep you need to support your mood and energy.

The Cycle of the Nervous System

Throughout the day, we automatically cycle through different states of the nervous system. This is referred to as Polyvagal Theory, a concept coined by Dr. Stephen Porges. Polyvagal Theory speaks to the nervous systems variety of responses controlled by the vagus nerve.

The vagus nerve is the on-off switch between the sympathetic nervous system being on alert or the parasympathetic nervous system supporting rest and relaxation.

When we feel calm, safe, and connected, we are experiencing the ventral vagal state. We are plugged into the parasympathetic nervous system in a helpful way. This is sometimes referred to as rest and digest. In a perfect world, we'd always hang out in this connected, mindful place. But, due to stressors and trauma triggers, we can escalate into fight, flight, freeze, or fawn.

Once the sympathetic nervous system kicks into high gear, our bodies harness the resources to take action and go to battle, or remove ourselves from the situation. This is known as fight or flight. Blood flow and bodily resources are rerouted to our arms and legs giving us super-strength. Our breath can become shallow and internal organ function slows.

Beyond that point, the body reaches a freeze state of parasympathetic nervous system shutdown in an effort to conserve resources. If these tactics don't avert the threat, the fawn response may come in as a way to appease the threat. Fawn often looks like people pleasing, lack of boundaries, difficulty saying no, and compliance.

The chart on the following page illustrates this process of activation in the nervous system. In the calm, connected, green zone of being in the ventral vagal state, we are connected to others and engaged with the world in a grounding way. When our sympathetic nervous system is activated, escalation into the orange zone of fight/flight follows. If that doesn't work, the nervous system shuts down in the blue zone, conserving energy to survive. One may also find themselves going directly from the purple zone to the blue zone if that is their habitual response.

These trauma responses get stored in the body and the brain. When traumatic events remain unprocessed, our body responds with reactions as if the trauma is still happening. Similar triggers continue to elicit these nervous system cycles, even in non-life-threatening situations. The resources in your mental health apothecary are the key to disrupting this process. If we don't take the time to heal these patterns, chronic stress and health issues may follow.

Polyvagal Theory

Activation Increases ↑ / **Deactivation** ↓

FREEZE/FAWN
- Dissociation
- Conservation of Energy
- Shame
- Collapse
- Immobility
- Numbness
- Shutdown
- Depression
- Hopelessness
- Raised pain threshold
- Preparation for death
- Helplessness
- Trapped

DORSAL VAGAL (Life Threat) — Hypoarousal

FIGHT/FLIGHT
- Rage
- Panic
- Anger
- Fear
- Irritation
- Anxiety
- Frustration
- Worry & Concern

SYMPATHETIC (Danger) — Hyperarousal

SOCIAL ENGAGEMENT
- Connection
- Oriented to the Environment
- Safety
- Calmness in Connection
- Curiosity/Openness
- Settled
- Compassionate
- Groundedness
- Mindful/in the present

VENTRAL VAGAL (Safety)

PARASYMPATHETIC NERVOUS SYSTEM
FREEZE/FAWN

This is a state of survival. The nervous system is conserving and preserving energy in order for our body to sustain and endure whatever it perceives as life-threatening. This state of shut-down impacts the body in the following ways:

Increases:

Fuel storage & insulin activity
Immobilization behavior (fear)
Endorphins that help numb and raise pain threshold
Conservation of metabolic resources

Decreases:

Facial expressions & eye contact
Social behavior
Attunement to human voice
Sexual responses
Immune response
Heart rate
Blood pressure
Temperature
Muscle tone
Depth of breath

SYMPATHETIC NERVOUS SYSTEM
FIGHT/FLIGHT

Gearing up to defend ourselves or run for our lives, the fight or flight response is concerned with prioritizing our energy resources to get us through the threat. Adrenaline and cortisol pump through our system, charging us with energy. Resources are directed away from internal processes and re-routed to our extremities for the quickest response. This activation impacts the body in the following ways:

Increases:

Blood pressure
Heart rate
Fuel availability
Adrenaline
Oxygen circulation to vital organs
Blood clotting
Pupil size
Defensive responses

Decreases:

Salivation
Relational ability
Immune response
Fuel storage
Insulin activity
Digestion

PARASYMPATHETIC NERVOUS SYSTEM
SOCIAL CONNECTION

Ideally, the nervous system returns to a state of homeostasis and calm connection. When we are in this state of being calm and relaxed, we remember our interconnectedness. Bodily resources are routed back towards running our internal processes. Our body and mind both benefit from being in this state due to the following:

Increases:

Digestion
Resistance to infection
Rest & recuperation
Health & vitality

Circulation to nonvital organs
Oxytocin (involved in social bond)
Ability to relate and connect
Breath & prosody in voice

Decreases:

Defensive responses

Reflection

What is a warning signal in your body that lets you know your nervous system is being activated?

Headache
Tightness in my chest
Tension in my shoulders
Clenching my jaw
Tummy trouble
Dissociation

Once you realize you are in **fight/flight** or **freeze/fawn**, engage with a regulation resource as you stay attuned to your body. This is called **introspection** - awareness of internal sensations, and it is one of our senses.

Regulation resources are sensory based interventions that help bring our nervous system back to the calm, connected, ventral vagal state.

Reflection

How do you feel inside as you calm down?

Do you need to shift gears and engage in a more active activity, perhaps running instead of walking?

What kind of movement would be helpful as you calm down from being in fight/flight or freeze/fawn?

What regulation resources were most effective for you?

What's your daily bandwidth?

Each day we begin with a limited amount of energy based on how we slept, our overall health, and stress levels. That bandwidth changes throughout the day and month based on variables impacting mental and physical health. People who live with chronic health conditions start the day with less energy than those who are able-bodied. People who live with mental health issues start the day with less energy than those who feel mentally well.

We can add to our energy by making choices that align with our personal needs. We deplete our energy by engaging in activities that are out of alignment with our values, or violate boundaries. Boundaries are the limits we set for ourselves and others. Maintaining boundaries and saying no to that which is beyond our bandwidth is self-preservation. Tapping into how much stress we can tolerate will help us get clear on what boundaries need to be set to protect our peace and stay well.

Another way to conceptualize this is called "Window of Tolerance." Termed by Dr. Dan Siegel, this is the ideal state for people to function and thrive in everyday life. Moving out of that window puts us back in fight/flight or freeze/fawn. Staying in the window of tolerance means an awareness of how much stress or sensory input we can handle, and choosing to manage our environment and stressors as best as possible.

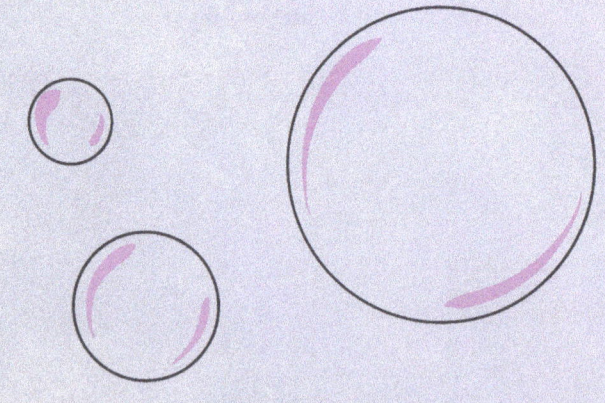

Activity

If you could put yourself in a protective bubble, what would you allow in, and what has to stay on the outside?

Saying yes to every activity offered
Charging less than my worth

Spending time with supportive friends
Saying yes to activities that fill my cup

Activity — Bandwidth: What makes the bubble smaller and what makes it bigger?

Restrictive activities.

drinking alcohol
lack of sleep
too much sensory input

Expansive activities

breathing practices
exercise
solid rest

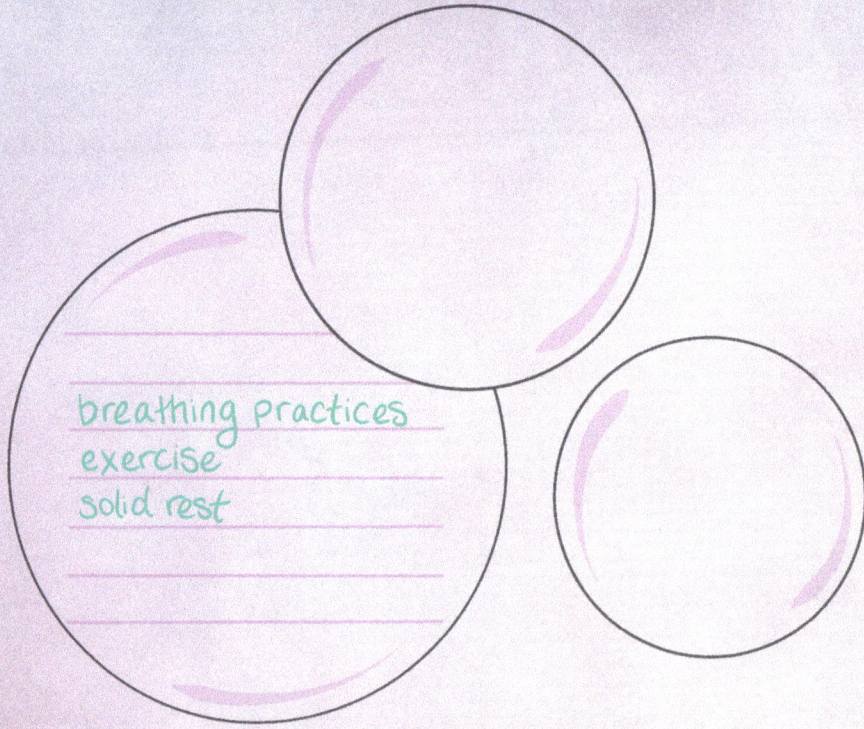

The Magic of Monthly Cycles

Each month contains two powerful cycles - the lunar cycle and the menstrual cycle. Interestingly, they share a similar cycle length of approximately 29.5 days. They both reach their peak energy on or around day 14 of each cycle. Due to hormonal fluctuations throughout the menstrual cycle, mood and energy levels change.

Synchronization and increased awareness of one's menstrual cycle and the moon phases can be a powerful way to connect with increased energy to make changes, reach goals, and heal. Research shows that menstruation often aligns with the full and new moon, suggesting that the Moon's gravitational pull when it is closest to the Earth acts as a cue toward our human body clock.

Honoring these cycles requires awareness of times when the body and nature want us to slow down, and ramping up when we have the energy available. Historically, women need rest before and during their cycle. This is a time to retreat. Coming out of that phase and moving toward ovulation is a time when we reemerge and regain energy. This then peaks at ovulation, a time of completion or manifestation and energy decreases again as the cycle completes. Hormone fluctuations have a powerful effect on our mood.

How the Moon impacts Mood

Each month, as the Moon orbits the Earth, we witness a similar cycle in the luminescence of the moon. When the moon is new, we are encouraged to rest and prepare. As the moon waxes and builds up to full, we gain energy. The full moon is the most fruitful time to manifest your desires, and as the moon wanes we slow down and retreat again. The moon follows a much slower cycle than the sun, balancing the Sun's fire energy with a rhythm that honors the significance of each phase.

Mood and sleep cycles are impacted by the moon. Research shows humans fall asleep later on nights when the Moon is full, and sleep is less restful.

Trying to align your goals, tasks, and responsibilities with the phases of the Moon or your cycle is a valuable experiment which we will explore in the following pages. Notice if you have more energy to complete certain tasks around ovulation or the full moon, and schedule time to rest around the new moon or whenever you feel most depleted during your menstrual cycle. How do you feel?

Every monthly cycle is a microcosm of the life cycle itself.

Take notice of your mood and energy levels at each point of either cycle and plan accordingly.

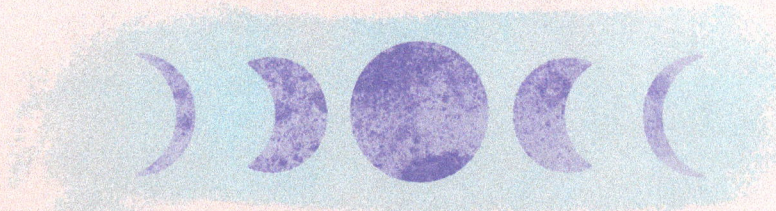

 **Activity**   **Self-Experiment**

Use the cycle tracker worksheets and key to record your menstrual cycle, the moon phases, how much you've slept, and your mood. Recording how you feel for three months in a row can help gather data about your patterns. That information is useful to prepare accordingly for events, plans, and projects that need more energy, and to rest, recover, and use resources when necessary.

For menstruating people, begin using the cycle tracker tool on the first day of your cycle. Day 1 is the first day the uterus lining begins to shed. If you do not menstruate, or if your cycle is a unique length, begin using the tracker on the new moon, and let the moon's phases be your guide. Once you've spent a few months recording, go back, compare notes, and answer the reflection questions.

This tool is meant as a container for your self-experiment in tracking how your mood, sleep and mental health change throughout the month. Whether you track using your cycle or the Moon, a few months of data will help you see patterns.

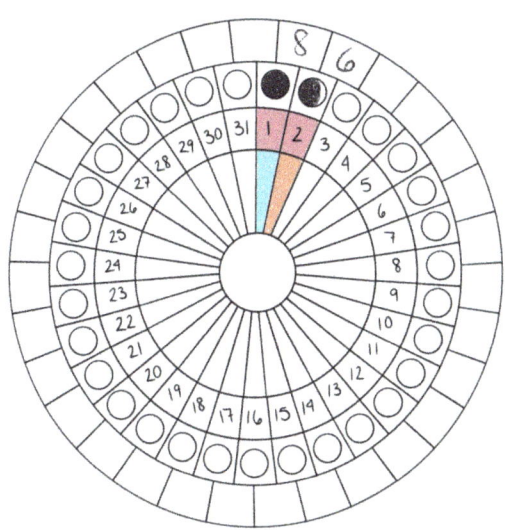

For additional copies of the cycle tracker, visit jamiehanley.com.
To track the moon phases, check out the Moon Phase app.
To track your cycle and the moon's phases, as well as hormonal fluctuations, moods and symptoms, the Stardust app is all encompassing.

Sleep/Menstrual/Moon/Mood/Physical Symptoms Cycle tracker

Directions:

Color the innermost circle or write in your mood

Use the numbered spaces to start recording on day 1 of your cycle

Use the circles to indicate the phase of the moon

Use the outermost circle to record how much sleep you got that night

It's important to realize not everyone has a regular cycle, this is meant as a tool to study your body's patterns.

■	Happy, Relaxed, Joyful	■	Sick, Unmotivated, Tired
■	Sad, Lonely, Depressed	■	Average, Okay, Good
■	Energetic, Motivated	■	Angry, Anxious, Grumpy

Reflect and journal
Rest and nourish
Take a walk in nature

Start new projects
Do some creative writing
Create a Vision Board

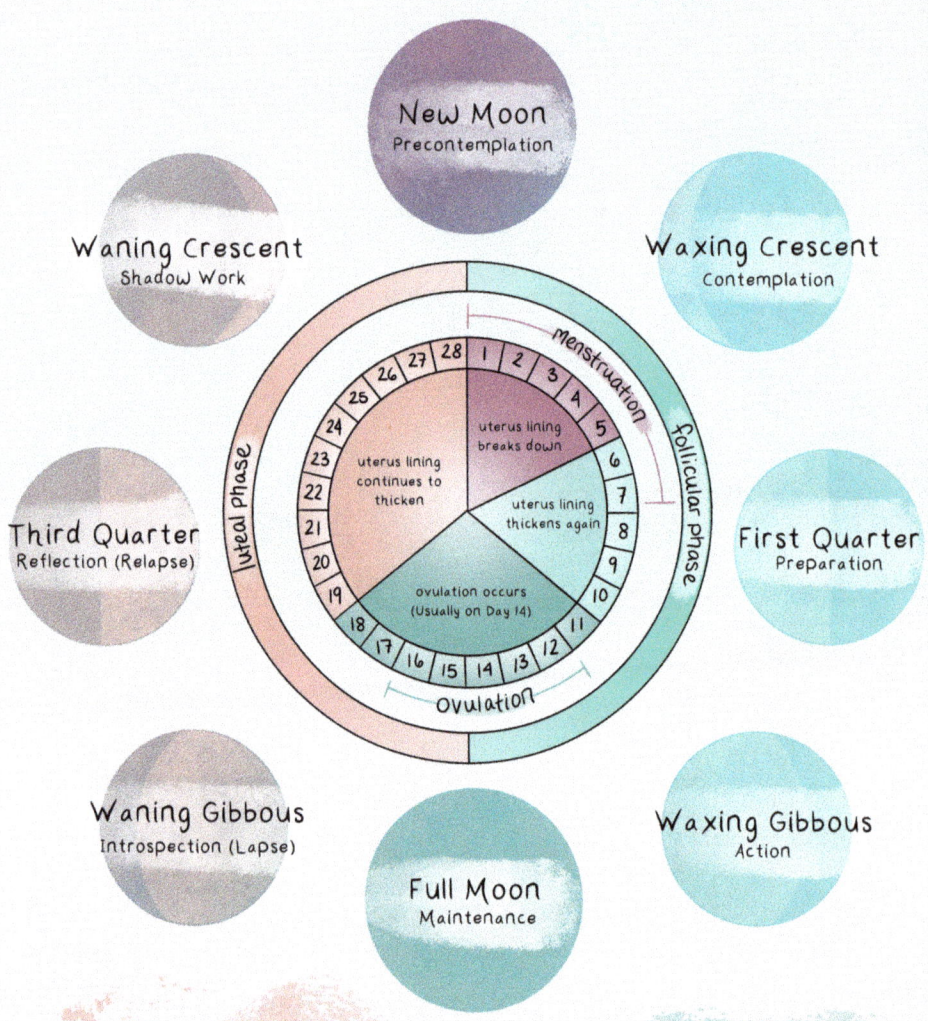

Practice self-care
Walk or do yoga
Wrap up projects

Try a new workout activity
Visit with friends
Give a presentation

Reflection

What responsibilities and activities require the most energy, and would benefit from being timed with ovulation/the full moon, when you feel most confident and energized?

What projects would benefit from the energy of the waxing moons, ramping up and building excitement?

What loose ends can you wrap up toward the end of this month during the waning moon phases?

How can you make the time and space for quiet rest during the new moon/menstruation phase?

The Magic of Seasonal Cycles

The seasons are another cyclical gift from Mother Nature. If you're blessed to live somewhere that the seasons shift, you know how impactful this can be on mood.

This annual, macro cycle is the big-picture version of the monthly cycle. Notice how your physical and mental health needs may shift depending on the season. This is unique to you and where you live.

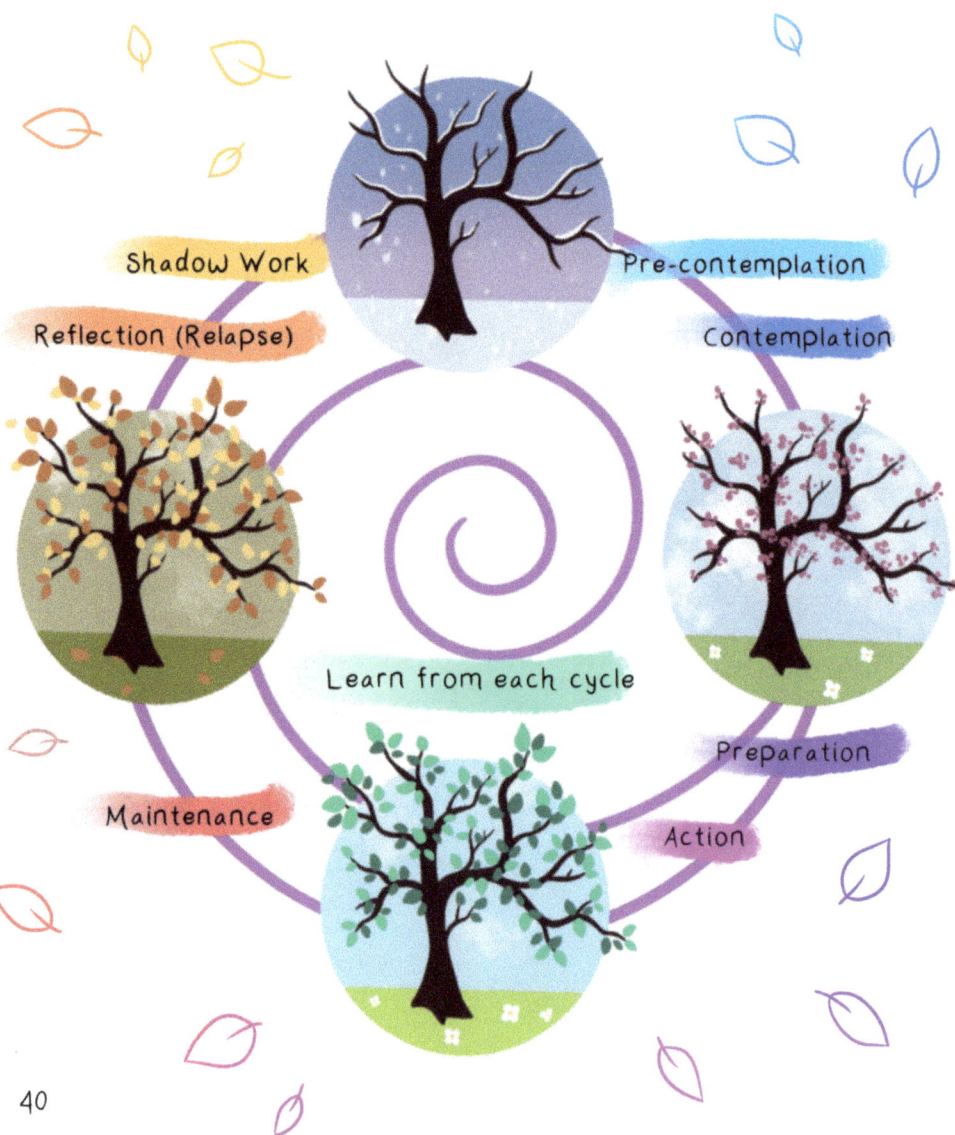

Winter, like the new moon, gives us the space and time to rest with shorter days and longer nights. It allows us to return to center and ground into the heavy earth and sometimes frozen water qualities of this season. The Danish and Norwegian concept of hygge is a beautiful way to lean into Winter. Hygge focuses on coziness, comfort, contentment, and connection, which are all beneficial for mental health.

Adaptive Winter Activities:

Sitting fireside, inside or out

S'mores

Reading

Wearing fuzzy socks

Sauna

Winter sports - skiing, snow shoeing, ice skating

Breath of fire to create heat

Warm/Hot Yoga

Getting outside during sunlight hours

Eating warm foods, soups, and comfort foods

Inquiries:

How can I slow down?

What can I do to make my environment more "warm and cozy?"

Where am I most content in Wintertime?

As the Earth awakens from her winter slumber, she brings the newness of Spring. Buds appear on the trees and let us know that they will bloom again. Rain nourishes the soil and welcomes perennial flowers. Birds return and baby animals appear. This is the time to plant physical, mental, and emotional seeds! Whether you begin a garden or begin a new project, Spring is the season of growth and emergence.

Adaptive Spring Activities:

- Garden, plant and pull weeds
- Start a new hobby
- Resume a creative activity - what did you enjoy in childhood?
- Spend time moving outside - biking, hiking, walking
- Take actionable steps in a new venture or project
- Eat seasonally and local - explore farmers' markets

Inquiries:

What do I want to bring forth in Spring?

What are updates I'm interested in making?

What is the first step in making these changes?

Where am I most content in Spring?

The bright, hot, longer days of summer can bring improved mood and increased energy to socialize. This season coordinates with the element of fire. It's a time when energy burns bright, and may even burn out. It's a time of rapid growth. This quality lends itself towards extroverted behavior, bringing projects, plans, and dreams into tangible form.

Adaptive Summer Activities:

- Cool off by the water
- Stay hydrated
- Soak up the longer days with lots of outside time (SPF protected, of course!)
- Water activities
- Consume cooling foods - ice cream, popsicles, raw fruits and veggies
- Beach time
- Adventures
- Travel
- Socializing

Inquiries:

What do I want to materialize this Summer?

How can I bring this into tangible form?

Where am I happiest in Summer?

What does my heart feel drawn to in Summer?

What are my passions?

The steamy Summer nights cool off into crisp Autumn mornings as the first harvest begins. The leaves turn, the blustery winds blow and the Earth prepares herself to rest. In Judaism and Paganism, the new year is celebrated in the Fall. This is the time to wrap up projects and put finishing touches on everything. This is the heart of harvest season, a fruitful time of completion.

Adaptive Autumn Activities:

- Enjoy seasonal foods like apples, pumpkin and squash
- Observe the beautiful changes in nature
- Get into the 'back to school' spirit by refreshing your home or office
- Become a student of something new
- Reflect on your accomplishments
- Connect with loved ones

Inquiries:

What accomplishments can I recognize during this harvest season?

How did I grow personally this year?

Where can I celebrate abundance in my life?

I am grateful for...

Once Autumn's harvest is complete it is time to rest again, returning to our caves to slow down, cozy up and hibernate for Winter. Making time to rest and allow for the decay and death of what no longer serves us is an important and valuable part of the process. Turning inward allows for time and space to evolve. In order to make room for anything new, we must be willing to let go and make space elsewhere.

Cycle of Change and The Seasons

Think of some big picture shifts and goals for the next year. How can you align your efforts towards these changes with the energy of the season? Use the questions below to gain clarity around your annual efforts toward change.

Winter

How can you make time to slow down and rest?
What ideas are sitting dormant?

Spring

What are you nurturing and growing?
How can you take the first step towards executing the idea?

Fall

What loose ends do you need to tie up?
What do you want to let go?
What did you learn from this experience?

Summer

How can you bring these efforts into tangible form?
What is a physical expression of this idea?

Equinox and Solstice Practices

There are various ways to observe the transition from one season to the next. Getting out in nature is one of the simplest and most effective ways to align with Mother Earth and the beauty of the seasons. You may want to refresh any alters in your home, or switch out seasonal decor.

The Summer Solstice is the longest day of the year, and marks the turning point for days to shorten again as we enter the most active, fiery season.

The Spring Equinox is a time to plant seeds in our gardens and grow our dreams and plans.

The Autumn Equinox ushers in the season of wind and intentions to release that which we no longer need.

The Winter Solstice marks the shortest day of the year, as well as the return of more sunlight each day. This is a time for rest and reflection.

Holidays

Reflect on the holidays of your country of origin or familial heritage.

How do these holidays fit into the seasons of the year?

What do they signify?

What traditions and foods are associated with these ancestral practices?

Many holidays across religions and cultures share similar meanings.

Magic lies in reconnecting with the unique traditions of our ancestors.

Identify seasonal traditions and rituals that resonate with you, and your lineage. Notice if seasonal decor updates feel adaptive to your mood. Whether associated with holidays or the season, it's an uplifting way to refresh your space. Attune to your seasonal cravings for changes in food, movement, and schedule and honor that intuitive guidance.

Activity

Take the reflections from the previous page and identify which practices resonate most with you. Choose three for each season and plan them out on the wheel below.

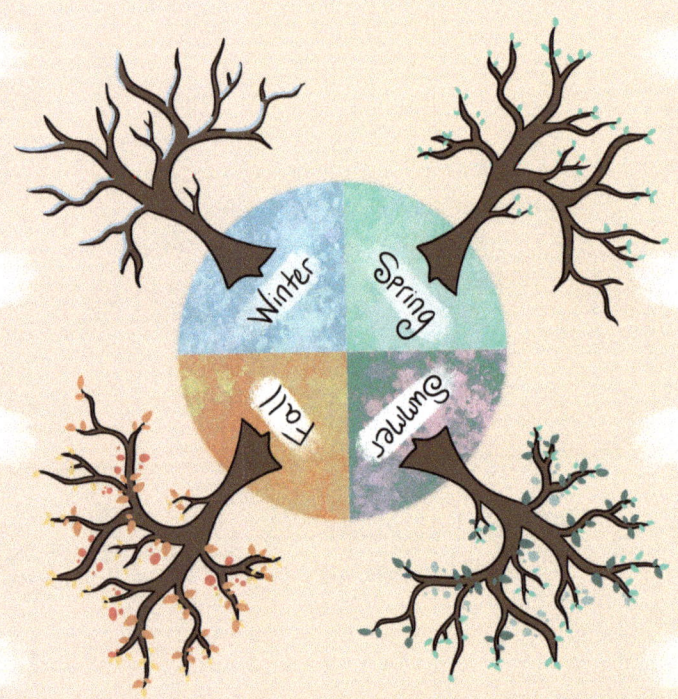

The Magic in our Life cycle

In our lifetime, we move through the phases of the Goddess. She embodies all the elements and all the seasons. As such, different forms of the Goddess show up as archetypes. Drawn from Jungian psychology, archetypes are symbols that have a universal understanding. Jung refers to them like a "universal fingerprint."

Traditionally, there have been three female archetypes of maiden, mother, and crone. However, the addition of a fourth archetype of wise woman between mother and crone accounts for women living longer and fuller lives. Awareness of these archetypes helps us gain insight into what needs are going unmet and the tasks of each phase of life.

You may notice yourself resonating with different archetypes in different situations. Perhaps there is an unmet need in a past phase that you want to revisit or heal. Trust that there is a greater collective unconscious and that your nervous system holds the answers for healing.

You are exactly where you are supposed to be.

Phases of the Goddess

Maiden

Waxing Moon
Follicular Phase
Spring

Tasks of the Maiden

Individuation
Self-discovery
Exploration
Growth

The Goddess in Maiden is beginning her journey. She is full of potential and budding with energy. The possibilities for her are endless and seeds are just being planted.

Where in your life are your planting seeds?

Mother

Full Moon
Ovulatory Phase
Summer

Tasks of the Mother

Introspection
Transformation
Creation
Nurturing

The Goddess in Mother is connecting to her highest potential for creation. She births, nurtures and grows in several aspects of her life.

Where are you manifesting, birthing and creating?

Wise Woman

Waning Moon
Luteal Phase
Autumn

Tasks of the Wise Woman

Teaching
Evolving
Reflection
Authenticity

The Goddess in Wise Woman uses the knowledge of her life to teach others. She may show up as a caregiver, teacher, helper, witch, or enchantress, focused on leaving her legacy.

Where are you sharing wisdom and creating a legacy?

Crone

New Moon
Menstruation Phase
Winter

Tasks of the Crone

Leaving a legacy
Sharing knowledge
Acceptance

The Goddess in Crone is closest to crossing over. As an elder she is a sage, revered for her wisdom. She fully trusts her intuition, and accepts that death is an inevitable aspect of life.

What can you accept that has come to an end?

Part 2

Resources by the light of the Moon

From here, we will move through the phases of the moon as they align with the emotional work, resources, and reflections that align with the energy of that moon phase.

New Moon
Set the Foundation of Caring and Tending to Yourself

In the stillness of the new moon, we set the groundwork for caring and tending to ourselves. While these foundational elements of self-care may seem basic, they have a tremendous impact on our well being.

Creating Conditions for Calm

We have the ability to resource our system, increasing resilience and reducing vulnerability to negative emotions. There are five important aspects to remember, as outlined in the PLEASE skill drawn from Dialectical Behavioral Therapy. These skills can make all the difference between feeling chaotic or calm.

Physical ILlness: It's exponentially challenging to manage your mood if you are sick or in pain. Be sure to address any physical symptoms and take medications as prescribed, for both physical and mental health. If you have a headache, and there's a certain type of medication that works for you, take it, or go lay down in a dark room and rest. If a prescription to support your mental health would be beneficial in order to use coping skills more effectively and that is in your best interest, go for it. Treat your body gently and take good care of it. You only get one!

List any physical symptoms you currently experience and treatment.

Schedule all annual doctors appointments and regular visits based on your needs.

Rule out any physical origins of mental health symptoms such as thyroid issues.

What physical health needs can you prioritize?

Eat Balanced: There are no good or bad foods - that's another example of all or nothing thinking. Reality is there's value in every food, whether it be from calories, nutritional content, taste, or enjoyment. Be sure you are eating a balance of foods that feel nourishing for both your body and mind. Notice what foods leave you feeling sluggish, and which help you feel energized. Notice what times work best for your meals to stave off getting "hangry."

What is an easy, nourishing meal for you?

What kind of snacks help you stay fueled?

What foods deplete your body?

What foods energize your body?

Avoid Mood-altering Drugs and Alcohol: While this seems self-explanatory, dominant culture and marketing tactics would have us believe that alcohol helps people relax and enjoy themselves. In reality, drugs and alcohol can amplify negative emotions. And while that first drink may feel relaxing because alcohol is a depressant, the brain gets tricked into thinking it needs alcohol above all else, which inevitably leads to more drinks. Alcohol also exacerbates anxiety symptoms and interrupts sleep, adding fuel to the fire of anxiety which can bring on an epic emotional hangover.

Caffeine is another common substance that can exacerbate anxiety, however it can also offer a positive energy boost and increased focus. Notice how much is right for you on a regular basis.

What substances do you currently use that impact your mood?

How do those substances impact your mood?

What would you like to change about your use of these substances?

Sleep: Most adults need 7 to 9 hours of sleep per night to feel well rested. Notice how much sleep you need, and adjust your bedtime and waking alarm to allow enough rest. Turn off screens an hour before bed if possible, or at least put them on night shift mode. What helps you relax at night? Do you prefer a shower before bed, or is that part of your morning routine? Perhaps a sleep meditation or gentle stretching before bed would help you relax. Above all, make sure you are setting yourself up for quality sleep, because cranky isn't just for kids - we all get cranky when sleep-deprived. Sleep is crucial for our mental health, and lack of sleep is guaranteed to exacerbate negative emotions and symptoms.

How many hours of sleep do you currently get?

How do you feel upon waking?

What works about your sleep routine?

What can you adjust?

Exercise: Whether you move for twenty minutes a day or thirty minutes four times a week, both have been shown to increase mood-supporting neurotransmitters and thus decrease anxiety and depression. Exercise is a natural way to improve mood and well-being. Whether you attribute it to distraction, mindfulness, community, or simply participating in a playful activity, the bottom line is that exercise is adaptive. So add some joyful movement to your days and welcome the good vibes.

What forms of movement do you truly enjoy?

What are reasonable expectations to integrate movement into your week?

What helps motivate you to exercise?

Coping using the Elements

The qualities of each element can play a powerful role in our self-care routine. When it comes to soothing ourselves as humans, the elements provide sensory input which our nervous system can register as relaxing or taxing. Knowing what your nervous system finds adaptive and healing is crucial.

Take time to explore self-care in the following categories.

Air
Notice your breath
Feel the breeze on your skin
Listen to the wind in the trees or the birds
Let out a sigh
Do an intentional breathing practice

_____
_____

Fire
Take a sauna
Enjoy a hot shower
Cozy up by the fire
Light a candle
Drink a warm beverage

_____
_____

Water

Draw a bath
Take a swim
Run your hands under cold water
Take a drink of cold water
Visit the beach

Earth

Walk barefoot and focus on your feet
Go hiking
Pause and notice the nature around you
Pay attention to where you connect to the earth

Track your habits and practices

In this section, you'll find a weekly self-care checklist to help you get a big picture sense of how you're tending to your mental health. Color the crystals to keep track of your daily routines, but there's no pressure to check off every item daily. Zoom out and get an overview of your self-care practices throughout the week. There is no right or wrong way to do this, as long as what you are doing is helpful for your physical and mental health.

Remember, you know yourself best!

Consider the following as you track your behaviors during the week:

- You are like a plant. You NEED water - approximately half your body weight in ounces each day. If you drink caffeine, increase your daily water intake by however much caffeine you drink.

$$\left[(\text{your body weight in lbs}) \div 2\right] + (\text{caffeine in oz}) = \text{the amount of } H_2O \text{ to drink daily}$$

- How many days a week do you want to move your body? Allow yourself days to rest when needed.

- View nutrition from a weekly perspective. Commit to nourishing your body. Don't give "bad days" or "bad foods" one more ounce of your precious energy.

- Aim for progress not perfection. Where do you see opportunities for growth?

- Compare yourself only to yourself. What do you engage with when you feel well?

- Consistent doesn't mean constant. Allow yourself to be imperfect in these practices. Some things may need your attention daily, others may be just a few times a week or less.

Self-care Checklist

(Color in the crystals)

	Sun	Mon	Tues	Wed	Thurs	Fri	Sat
Drink water	◇	◇	◇	◇	◇	◇	◇
Eat balanced	◇	◇	◇	◇	◇	◇	◇
Take medications & vitamins	◇	◇	◇	◇	◇	◇	◇
Move joyfully	◇	◇	◇	◇	◇	◇	◇
Tidy your space	◇	◇	◇	◇	◇	◇	◇
Do something creative	◇	◇	◇	◇	◇	◇	◇
Engage in a spiritual practice	◇	◇	◇	◇	◇	◇	◇
Connect with a loved one	◇	◇	◇	◇	◇	◇	◇
Spend time in nature	◇	◇	◇	◇	◇	◇	◇
Go to therapy	◇	◇	◇	◇	◇	◇	◇

I am Grateful for...

Know your personality

Investigating whether you are an introvert, extrovert, or ambivert and examining your social battery is extremely valuable information.

Introverts need time alone to recharge their social battery. They don't dislike people, however they become depleted if they need to be social for a long period of time, interact with people they don't know, or are put in uncomfortable situations. They might keep a close knit circle of friends.

Extroverts feel energized when spending time with others. Nothing fills them up more than endless hours of connection with friends, family, and new acquaintances. They're outgoing and love to socialize. They may also enjoy entertaining, planning events and gatherings.

Many people are ambiverts and have a mix of qualities of both personality types. This can also depend on the time of year or time of month. Summer is a season of extroversion, while Winter is the season of introversion. These personality traits exist on a spectrum, and where you land is mobile.

Introvert —————— Ambivert —————— Extrovert

Quiz   To get a better sense of whether you are an introvert, extrovert, or ambivert, answer the quiz below:

When invited to a social gathering, I will:
A Immediately reach out to friends and start planning my outfit.
B Wait to RSVP until the date gets closer and see how I feel.
C Get exhausted just thinking about it.

At social gatherings, I'm most comfortable
A Fluttering around like a social butterfly.
B Hanging close to the people I know and love.
C Chillin by the snacks.

When managing a personal issue, I prefer to
A Talk it out with a few sources to get different points of view.
B Connect with a trusted friend or therapist.
C Think it through on my own.

If presented with a public speaking opportunity
A I am psyched! Getting up in front of a crowd is my jam!
B I can do it, but I'll have to be well resourced.
C Hell no! Not a chance.

Group projects are
A So much fun! I love working together and might even be the group leader.
B Tolerable. Not my favorite thing, but I'll survive.
C A headache. I'd rather work on my own.

Mostly A's - You're an extrovert. The life of the party, you thrive on being around people.
Mostly B's - You're an ambivert. The best of both worlds, you can flow between extroversion and introversion as needed.
Mostly C's - You're an introvert. You need intentional alone time in order to thrive.

Assess Your Social Battery

How much social time do you need on a weekly basis?

I feel well-resourced when I socialize _____ times a week.

How much time do you spend with yourself?

What kinds of social situations fill your heart up?

What social situations leave you drained?

Where do you get your social needs met?

Activity

As an introvert, if your social battery is drained, the indicator light is on that you need to fuel up the tank.

What solo activities from your resource bank help you fill your tank?

Arts and crafts

Listening to music

Walking at the beach

As an extrovert, if your social battery is drained, fueling up may involve group activities and getting out more.

Who do you want to connect with and how?

◊ Find a team sport

◊ Go out dancing with friends

◊

◊

◊

Waxing Crescent
Contemplating Change

As a sliver of the waxing crescent Moon lights the night sky, we consider the process of change. Change doesn't happen overnight, but in stages, over the course of time. Change is the only constant.

The Cycle of Change and Phases of the Moon

Reflect back to the cycle of change model we met on page 11. The process of the cycle of change and the quality of each phase is supported by Moon energy. By connecting with the energy of each aspect of the Moon, we align our intentions to change or create with this monthly process. We co-create with the Moon as our supportive guide. Some processes may take several months and multiple cycles, others may take just one month.

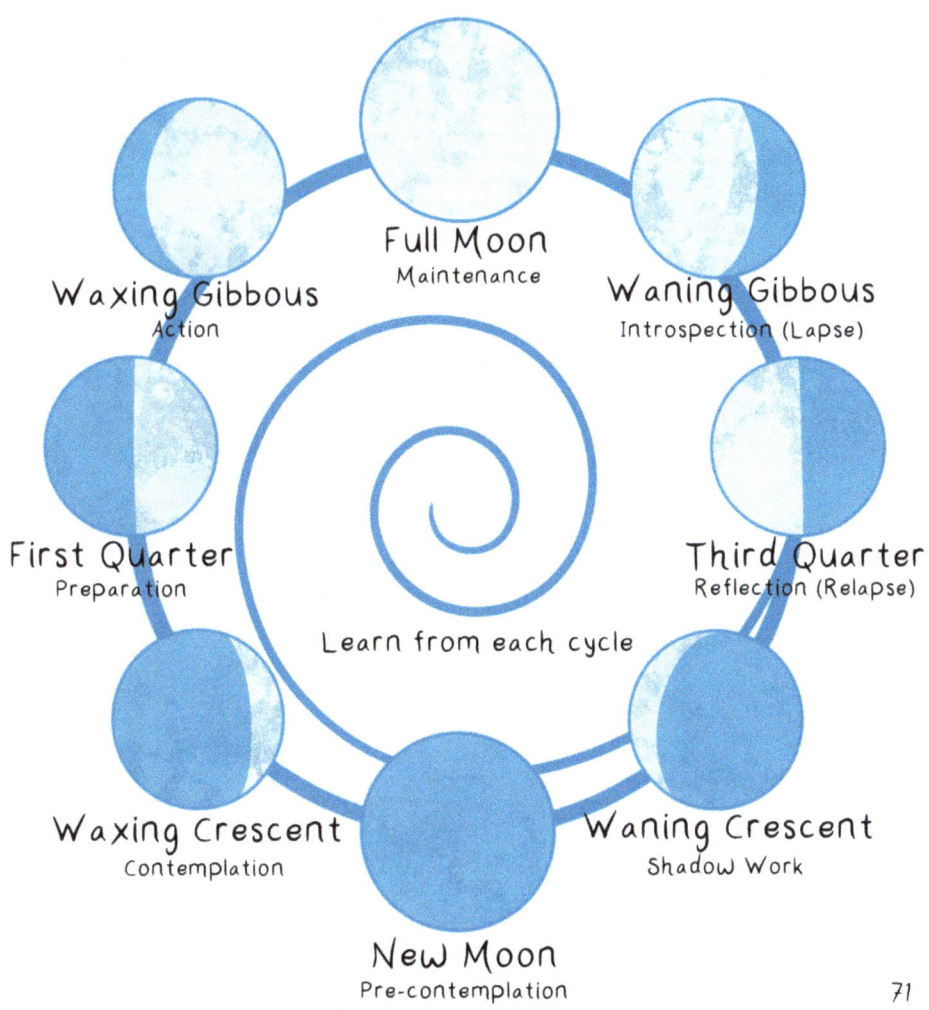

Reach for the Stars and Co-create with the Moon

When you align the energy of the Moon with the stages of change in order to plan, grow, reach for the stars and meet your goals, a natural process of production and reflection occurs. Use the following pages to map out a goal for this month.

What are some goals, plans, or dreams currently sitting dormant? What would you like to heal within yourself?

Pre-contemplation
New Moon

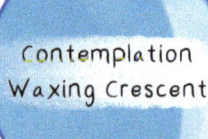

Why do you want to work on it? What will this entail?

Contemplation
Waxing Crescent

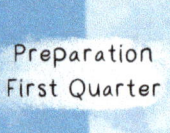

What first step can you take to create some momentum?

Preparation
First Quarter

Take the first step! Do the hard thing! How do you feel?

Action
Waxing Gibbous

Maintenance — Full Moon
What is the next step towards your goal? What will it take for you to continue to work on this?

Introspection — Waning Gibbous
What were you able to execute that was within your control?

Reflection — Third Quarter
How has your plan panned out thus far?

Shadow Work — Waning Crescent
What negative, limiting beliefs are barriers to my goals? How can I resolve them?

Garden of Wellness

Take a look at the "Garden of Wellness" below. Each flowerpot represents an aspect of your life. Draw plants and flowers in the pots to represent how you are doing with meeting your own needs in that area. Consider the type of plant or flower that best represents how you feel, its phase of growth (seed, stem, leaves, etc.), and how abundantly it grows. How will you nurture your Garden of Wellness?

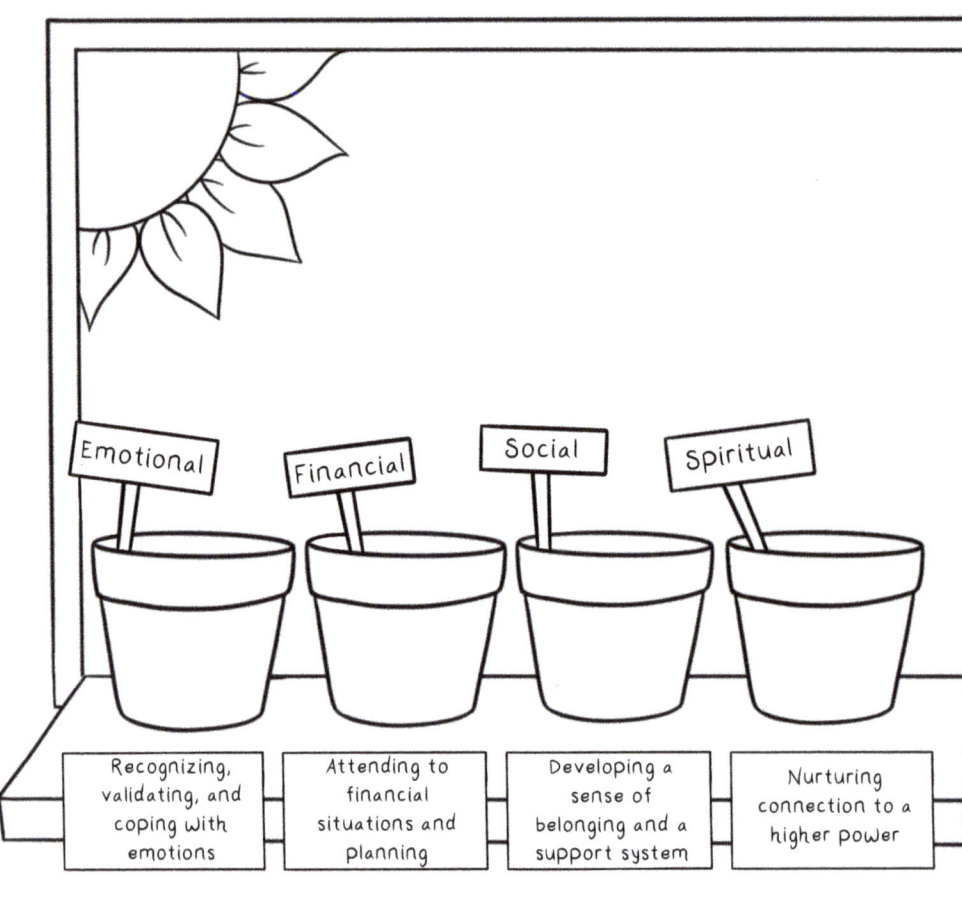

Pros and Cons to Change

Change is uncomfortable. We continue our habitual ways of coping for a reason. Take a moment to consider what you might lose if you don't change and what you might gain from changing.

Changing

Pros:	Cons:

Staying the same

Pros:	Cons:

Radical Acceptance

We are constantly navigating change, juggling, and adapting as we evolve again and again through each of these patterns. Each time we complete a revolution, we get the opportunity to start again. When we align our energy with that of the natural cycles around us, we tap into a flow state that supports and honors our energy and mood.

Aligning with the cycles of nature requires radical acceptance: Accepting the reality of our current situation, instead of wishing it was some other way.

For example: If you think "I hate winter," and spend all winter wishing it was summer, you'd be pretty miserable. However, if you notice "Hey, it's winter again. In the winter, my mood gets worse from the dark and cold," then you have choices. There are options, like moving somewhere warm or creating adaptive practices to enjoy the winter more, such as snowshoeing and embracing all things cozy.

When it comes to our mental health and wellness, we are impacted by these cycles. Resisting fluctuations, shifts, and change only causes us more suffering. If we resist the flow of these evolutionary healing experiences, we deprive ourselves of the growth that can only come from being present with uncomfortable feelings.

ACCEPTING our PRESENT MOMENT REALITY can reduce our SUFFERING

Radical acceptance is a practice. Once you've recognized what you are resisting, you need to accept it over and over and over again. Acceptance does not necessarily mean you agree, support, or approve of the situation. However, by accepting the reality of the situation you are able to take the next step on your journey. Freedom from denial will open the path for forward momentum.

Exercise for practicing Radical Acceptance:

Take a moment to sit and center yourself.
Take three deep belly breaths, and consider the following:

What do I need to accept?

On a scale of 1-10, how distressing does this feel currently?

Where do I notice resistance to accepting reality?

What am I avoiding accepting?

Where do I notice tension in my body?

Once you've realized what needs your acceptance, sit with this reality.

Relax the places where you notice tension.

Breathe deeply again and hold this reality in your mind and in your heart as you offer yourself compassion, patience, and kindness.

Practice for at least five minutes, then check back with your distress level and notice any changes.

Practice however many rounds of radical acceptance you need to reduce your suffering.

After practicing radical acceptance, how distressed are you on a scale of 1-10?

It can be helpful to start practicing radical acceptance with something less activating for the nervous system, like the weather in the example above. Once you get a sense of how radical acceptance works, move on to more challenging situations.

First Quarter
Identify and add External Resources

As the half moon lights the sky, she gains energy and brightness. When we identify resources and apply them with intention, we gain energy and brightness as well.

Resources

Resources help us to cope more effectively. They can exist within us or be related to something outside of us. By resourcing ourselves we are essentially adding tools to our coping skills toolbox. It's like investing in our nervous system's bank account every time you make the intentional choice to practice supporting your mental health.

Resources can be internal or external. Internal resources are coping skills that exist within ourselves, as well as our sense of self-worth. External resources are skills that require us to engage with something outside of ourselves.

For example, diaphragmatic breathing is an internal resource. I can do it and nobody notices and I don't need anything outside of myself to engage in that coping skill.

Gardening is an external resource because I need to be in my yard to work in my garden.

The friends and family that make up your support network are external resources as well.

External resource: Creative Arts Practices

Whether you paint, color, craft, crochet, knit, or have an eye for photography, get creative!

Maybe you love music, singing, dancing, writing, or redecorating. You don't have to be amazing at whatever it is, just give it a try! With practice you'll improve which is good for self-esteem.

There is therapeutic value in being creative without any expectations as a form of embracing imperfection.

Is there a creative outlet from your childhood that you've abandoned since adulting took over?

Any creative endeavors you've been curious to try?

What kind of creativity inspires you?

How can you bring more creativity into your life?

External resource:

Creating my village of support

Work smarter, not harder. Simplify. Get tasks off your plate and off your mental load. Trust me - you don't want to take on the world on your own. Create a village that supports your visions, your dreams, your family, and the life you want for yourself.

Consider the following questions to streamline your life:

What has you feeling overwhelmed at work or home?

Who can you ask for support or partnership?

What tasks do you dread?

Who can take over these tasks?

Who is a compassionate, active listener?

Who can you turn to when you need to "dump-out" to a subjective party?

Who shares your values?

This may seem luxurious, but it can be life - changing if your time is better spent elsewhere. Think about solutions like a meal prep service, grocery delivery or online orders, or a cleaning service every few weeks. Hold conversations about equity amongst adults in regards to household chores. Enlist supportive family and friends. Build your village in any way possible. Look to family and friends to be supportive without expecting any one person to meet all your needs.

Activity

My Village of Support

On the mailbox sign write the name of a supportive person in your life.

On the arrows, list opportunities to ask for support or delegate.

External resource:

Therapy

Everyone can benefit from therapy! Clearly, I'm partial to this introspective work and the self-awareness that accompanies willingness to look within. Whether you attend counseling weekly, bi-monthly, or whenever you need to check in, there is value in processing the human experience with a non-judgmental source of support.

A trusting therapeutic relationship is the foundation of healing work, which then allows us to be vulnerable and work towards accepting both the positive and less desirable aspects of our personalities. All emotions and experiences are welcome in the therapy room as they are valid and valuable tools for self-study.

There are several different types of therapy approaches, ranging from very structured with homework to creative approaches or talk therapy. Treatment episodes can be short or long. You may need to investigate different styles or meet with a few therapists until you find the right fit.

Person Centered Therapy - Ideally all therapy is centered on the client's goals and needs. Therapy is all about YOU.

Cognitive Behavioral Therapy - CBT invites us to challenge the thoughts that cause emotional and behavioral responses. It centers on mindfulness.

Dialectical Behavioral Therapy - DBT gets clients away from black and white thinking and helps them consider all the possibilities in a situation.

Eye Movement Desensitization and Reprocessing - A body based form of trauma treatment, EMDR helps process the memories that keep our nervous system stuck in a trauma response.

Sand Tray Therapy - This creative approach uses symbolic figures placed in a sandbox to tell stories that access the unconscious and subconscious mind.

Art Therapy - Art therapists guide clients to use creative mediums such as paint or clay to process their emotions and experiences.

Dance Therapy - Dance therapy incorporates movement to process emotions and integrate experiences.

Somatic Therapy - Any kind of therapy that addresses the mind-body connection and their impact on each other, such as yoga, meditation, or somatic experiencing.

Group Therapy - Group therapy brings several clients together for a common goal. They can be psychoeducational, skill, or process-based.

Waxing Gibbous
Add and Strengthen Internal Resources

Just as the Moon grows, we grow. When we look within, gain insight, and learn about ourselves, we are able to be more intentional with our choices.

Distorted Thoughts

Sometimes our mind plays tricks that cause us to think in unhealthy ways. There are several common ways our thoughts deceive us, causing a spiral of negative mental and physical health responses.

Remember, your nervous system responds to your thoughts!

Take a look at the unhelpful thinking styles below and begin to notice where your thoughts create more suffering.

All or Nothing Thinking is only seeing the extremes in a situation. For example, "My artwork must be perfect or it's not worth doing at all." Someone who engages in these thought patterns has difficulty recognizing the spectrum of possibilities.

Do you label your emotions as good or bad?
Do you have a "love it" or "hate it" attitude towards activities, interests, or people?
Do you label actions as right and wrong?

Remedy - Zoom out to observe the situation from all sides, move away from extremes and more towards the middle. This creates freedom to consider many possibilities and accept that multiple opinions can be true. This is dialectical thinking, and is the basis for Dialectical Behavior Therapy.

Focusing on the Negative aspects of a situation by disqualifying or filtering out the positive aspects or over-generalizing the entire experience as negative is another example of thinking in extremes that causes suffering. This shows up in situations like fixating on negative feedback in a work review and disregarding anything positive. Another example is when someone does really well on a test, however can't get past the few questions they missed.

Do you find yourself ruminating on the negative parts of an experience?
Do you have difficulty recognizing your positive attributes and strengths?
Are you able to recognize your efforts and take credit for your work?

Remedy - Look at both the successes and areas for improvement in any given situation

Jumping to Conclusions is assuming what others are thinking or trying to predict the future. You have NO idea what is going on in someone's life. We can't read minds or tell the future. Projecting forward or guessing about what someone is thinking is a futile effort, as we have no evidence for these conjectures.

Do you make assumptions about others that lead to more suffering?
Do you ruminate on others' opinions of you?

Remedy - Ask yourself, where's the evidence? Oftentimes, there's none!

Catastrophising is increasing the severity of a situation while **Minimizing** makes it seem less important. When someone catastrophizes, they jump to the absolute worst possible scenario. This can become very distressing when someone perseverates on the most negative possible outcome. **Minimizing** is the opposite, and occurs when someone downplays their feelings or the severity of a situation.

Do you ruminate about the worst possible outcome?
Is your response to distressing situations in proportion to the stressor?
Do you downplay your emotions or brush issues aside?

Remedy - Check the facts. Is your emotional response in proportion to the severity of the situation?

Using Emotional Reasoning is turning our feelings into facts, for example, "I made a silly mistake therefore I'm stupid," or "I feel lonely therefore I have no friends." Turning our feelings into facts leads to further suffering and distress. Just because we feel a certain way, doesn't mean it is true, The feeling itself is a real experience, but our brain can hook into that and jump to extremes.

Do you justify your behavior based on your emotions?
Do you turn your feelings into facts?

Remedy - Find Wise Mind by validating your feelings and emotional experience while checking the facts. Make an informed decision on your behaviors after looking at both sides.

Being Overly Critical of oneself is using words like "should" or "must" that reinforce unrealistic expectations of the self and others. When we think things should be different, we deny our current reality and cause ourselves to suffer more. Every time we "should" on ourselves, we reinforce negative beliefs around our own inadequacy. When you think, "I should call them more," you reinforce the belief you are an inadequate friend.

When do you find yourself using the word "should?"
How do you feel when you "should" all over yourself?
How does it feel to accept the current circumstances instead?

Remedy - Don't should on yourself!

Labeling oneself or others in a negative or critical way is overgeneralizing one trait or aspect of that person. For example, "She responded curtly, therefore she's a bitch." Or "He was late, therefore he is irresponsible." Notice when you make broad generalizations based on one experience.

Do you take opinions to the extreme based on one trait, experience, or situation?

Remedy - Remember, no person or experience can be defined by one trait or interaction. Validate your feelings - they may be warning you to proceed with caution. Everyone's opinions are valid and we don't always have to agree.

Personalizing is accepting fault with a situation unrelated to you. For example, when a friend is in a bad mood and you assume they are mad at you. You ask and it turns out they are tired.
Additionally, personalizing shows up as apologizing for things that are not your fault.

Do you find yourself feeling guilty or responsible for the actions of others?
Are you able to accept responsibility for your own actions when appropriate?

Remedy - Check the facts of the situation. If you need confirmation, check in with a trusted source of support. Take that feedback at face value.

Wise Mind

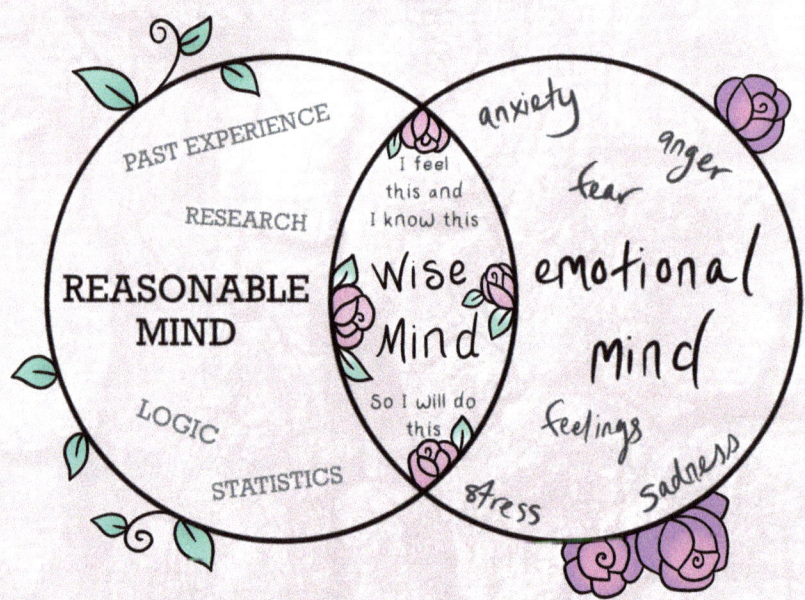

Seeking Wise Mind is another term for finding the gray area. It's the idea of zooming way out and realizing that there is no right or wrong, and that all possibilities are valid. So when you get yourself stuck in perfectionism, judgment, or extremes - pause, breathe, and try to find your flexible, Wise Mind by asking yourself the questions below.

1) Bring a challenging situation to mind. Check in with your emotions. What are they trying to tell you? Validate your emotions, as only you know how you feel!

2) The feelings are very real, but they may not be factual. Now, check in with the facts of the situation. What do you know to be true? What have you learned from past experience? Who can you touch base with for a reality check?

3) Validate your emotions and check the facts to come back to center before you make your next move. Notice how you respond to situations when you are in Wise Mind, as opposed to a heightened, emotional state of mind. How do you want to show up?

Boundaries

Healing requires awareness of boundaries. Boundaries can be time based, energetic, physical, and emotional. Exploring boundaries means knowing your limits regarding how much of your - time, energy, and efforts are required in any given situation.

Do you find youself saying "yes" to things and feeling resentful or drained afterword?

Can you identify a relationship where you make more of an effort than the other person?

When do you put your needs on the back burner?

What social and emotional needs do you have in different relationships?

Choose to prioritize yourself as often as possible. Take a long exhale, and watch the world begin to shift.

Keep saying "yes" to yourself - to your big dreams, relationships and interests that fill your cup.

Stay consistent in that resounding, unapologetic "yes" in order to show up as the best version of yourself as often as possible.

Of course we have obligations and we want to show up to support others. By working with boundaries, you'll learn how to reprioritize the time and energy you allot for yourself.

My Solar System of Boundaries & Relationships

Take a look at the solar system image on the next page. Place yourself in the center as the Sun.

Who are the people in your solar system? Who are you closest to, and who needs to be placed farther away?

Draw lines that connect you to your support system that also symbolize the quality of that relationship. Encircle each planet with a visual representation of the boundaries you hold with that person. Perhaps you want to use jagged, dashed, dotted, loopy lines, or any other pattern that resonates with you.

Notice where you have rigid boundaries and where boundaries are porous. Rigid boundaries are non-negotiable, like castle walls. Porous boundaries are often accompanied by people pleasing behaviors. and show up when we say yes to things that aren't in alignment with our values.

Where do you want to tighten up boundaries?

What can you say "no" to?

If you want to deepen a relationship, is there a boundary wall you need to lower?

Where can you be more vulnerable?

If we constantly expect ourselves to show up in our lives in the same way no matter what the variables - we set ourselves up for failure.

Essentially, give yourself grace.

Locus of control

Consider that which is within your control and that which is outside of your control. A sense of agency can quell anxiety, but reality is that most of our lived experience is outside of our grasp. The actions of others, life circumstances, and the weather are just a few examples of external locus of control. Accept that which you cannot control and turn your attention within.

This is called our internal locus of control.

You only have control over yourself, your own actions, and your choices.

Notice urges to control others or manipulate situations when you experience anxiety.

How does this show up for you?

What can you do to turn your awareness to your internal locus of control and sense into where you have agency?

Cope Ahead Plan

Print more copies at jamiehanley.com

Imagine/describe an event:

What is within my control?

What is outside of my control?

List what coping skills you need to use to manage the anticipated situation:
_____

Practice the scenario in your head and imagine it going well.

Who can I ask for help/support?

Anxiety Is My Superpower

Our emotions show up for a reason, each one has a purpose.

Anxiety shows up to protect us, keep us alive, and help us survive.

On the flip side, notice if there are times when your emotional or physical reactions seem out-of-proportion to the intensity of the problem. That's a sign anxiety is driving the behavior train and that you may want to check the facts or confer with a trusted source of support.

Sensing whether you feel frenetic or centered in your body will help you determine next action steps.

Full Moon
Time to shine!

Do the big, scary things you've been avoiding - it's probably exactly what you need! Collaborate and co-create with the big, bright energy of the full moon. Go all in with whatever action steps you've taken. Keep practicing and encourage yourself. Make changes and push beyond your comfort zone.

Do the Things that Scare you

Approach rather than avoid those daunting goals and projects. The only way out is through. Tackle these challenges head on while you are well resourced and have energy. The more you approach rather than avoid, the easier these anxiety provoking situations will become.

Be Your Own Cheerleader

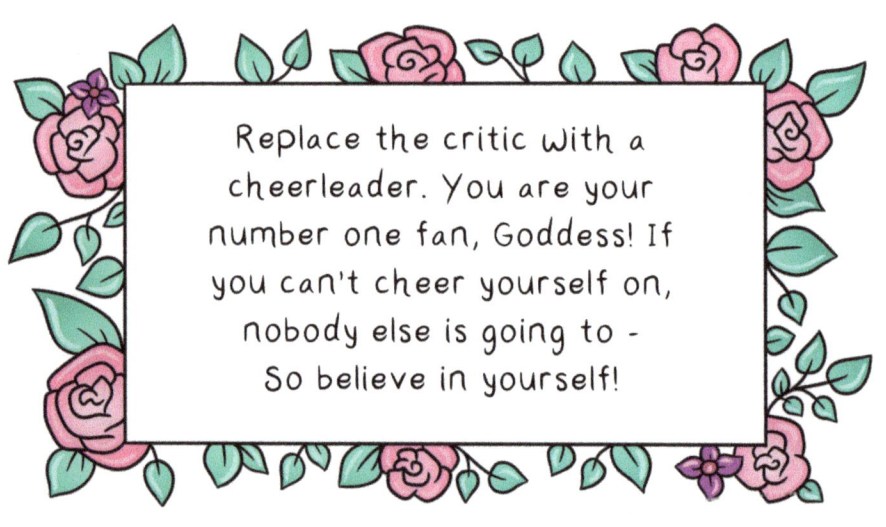

Replace the critic with a cheerleader. You are your number one fan, Goddess! If you can't cheer yourself on, nobody else is going to - So believe in yourself!

How can you cheer yourself on?

What affirmations do you need?

What is your motivation?

What creative outlets inspire you?

Affirmations

Affirmations are a powerful tool for shifting your mindset and moving in the direction of your goals. Use the prompts below to create affirmations unique to you. Write or post them in places where you'll see them regularly like a bathroom mirror, work whiteboard, or phone screen background for a daily reminder.

I am _____

I accept _____

Today I will focus on _____

I choose to release _____

I welcome _____

I believe in _____

It's okay to _____

I am grateful for _____

Waning Gibbous
Authentic Communication and Assertiveness

While the energy of the moon is starting to wane, keep showing up as your most authentic self. Apply the insight and skills you've gained to continue moving in the direction of your dreams. This means practice being assertive.

Effective Communication

When asserting yourself in any given situation, it's important to have an understanding of types of communication. Imagine a continuum of communication that spans from passive to aggressive.

Passive ← Assertive → Aggressive

Passive communication isn't speaking up for yourself. It's allowing yourself to get bulldozed, and can leave you feeling like a doormat. Passive-aggressive communication sends mixed messages, while someone might say they are "fine," their body language reads differently.

Aggressive communication is the other extreme, where someone is so pushy or loud they take up all the air and space in the room.

Assertive communication is in the middle, where one can ask for their needs and clearly communicate.

One of my favorite skills for practicing assertiveness is DBT's DEAR MAN.

Here's an example of how to use the DEAR MAN assertive communication skill to prepare for a challenging conversation where you have to ask for or say no to something. Be sure to do your homework before making an ask so you're prepared, and be sure the person you are asking has the ability to meet this need.

In this example, one partner has to ask the other to contribute more equally to the housework.

D: Describe the situation, just using the facts to start.

I've done all the laundry, dishes, and most of the cleaning and cooking after work this week.

E: Express your feelings using I statements.

I'm exhausted and feeling frustrated about how much time it takes away from downtime.

A: Ask clearly for what you need.

I really need to take one of these tasks off my plate. Can you take ownership of something?

R: Reinforce how what you're asking will benefit both parties.

If you take over one of these tasks, then we will have more time to spend together relaxing. We would also be modeling equity in the household which is important to us.

M: Be Mindful of staying on topic and discussing the current situation.

I just don't have the time right now to have ownership of all the household chores.

A: Act confident. Make eye contact, stand up tall, use a confident tone, take up space with your body, and don't apologize for your ask!

(Remind yourself there's nothing to be sorry about here!!!)

N: Negotiate. Be willing to meet in the middle, and ask if the other person has any suggestions!

D: Describe the situation, just using the facts to start.

E: Express your feelings using I statements.

A: Ask clearly for what you need.

R: Reinforce how what you're asking will benefit both parties.

M: Be mindful of staying on topic and discussing the current situation.

A: Act confident. Make eye contact, stand up tall, use a confident tone, take up space with your body, and don't apologize for your ask!

N: Negotiate. Be willing to meet in the middle, and ask if the other person has any suggestions!

Conscious Communication

The following skills are meant to support deeper, more meaningful communication. It can be beneficial to ask what someone needs in conversation - a good listener, advice, or problem solving, so as to set expectations around the conversation.

Validation

Validation lets another person know you understand them. Usually it's accomplished by reflecting what someone says, rephrasing their perspective, or finding an emotion word that describes their feelings. Validation doesn't mean you agree; it simply confirms that you understand.

Active Listening

Active listening and validation go hand-in-hand. You must be mindfully listening in order to validate someone. Notice when you are half-listening, distracted by thoughts of your side of the argument or how you relate. Often when we are listening to someone, we are distracted thinking about our own stuff! When this comes up, mindfully bring your attention back to the speaker.

Use "I statements"

When in conflict, speak to your feelings about a situation, instead of blaming the other person. Own your part in whatever is happening. Someone will likely be more receptive to "I feel calmer when the house is clean," as opposed to "You make me mad when you make a mess!"

Third Quarter
Make time for rest and reflection

Turning inward further, notice how you treat yourself. You can choose to treat yourself kindly or bully yourself with limiting negative beliefs. It's up to you. In the third quarter, consider what it would be like to treat yourself with tenderness.

Self-Compassion

Many of us anxious goddesses are walking around with a rude inner-critic fueled by negative beliefs. This voice magnifies anxiety and self-doubt, which keeps us playing small and tricks us into staying in our comfort zone. Ultimately, it can keep us from sharing our magic and gifts with the world.

This can show up in all kinds of ways throughout our lives. Maybe it causes doubt in your career or school, love, or friendships.

Notice when this negative self-talk appears and instead commit to speaking to yourself in a gentler tone. Think about how you would talk to a loved one, and how dear friends and family speak to you. Use that same tone when you speak to yourself - one of kindness, understanding, and compassion.

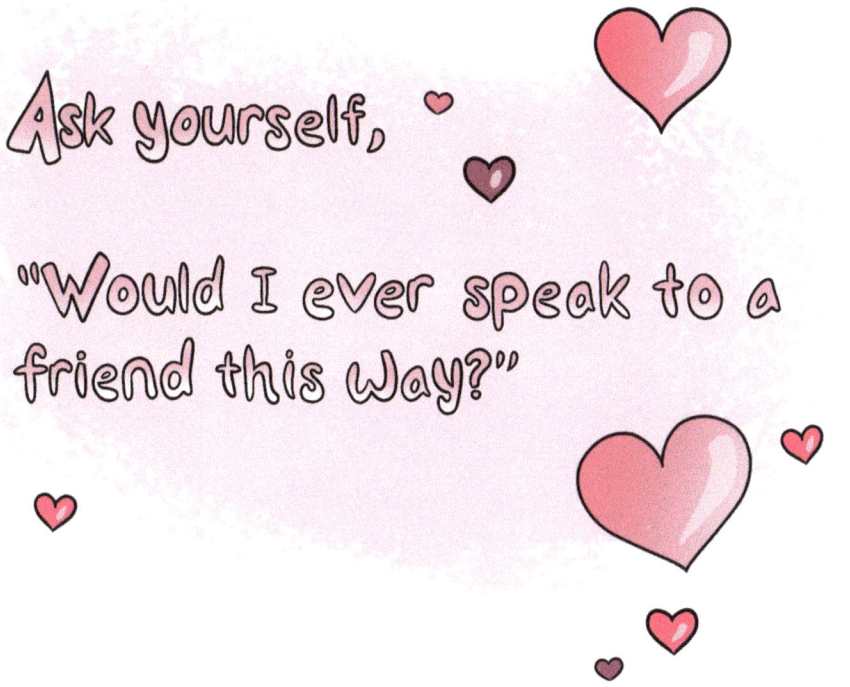

Ask yourself, "Would I ever speak to a friend this way?"

Metta: Loving Kindness Meditation

Metta is a Buddhist meditation practice that brings one into a state of compassion towards even the most difficult people in our lives. It can be adapted to choose the language that you find most healing. A simple yet profound version follows.

Bring to mind someone you love very dearly. Holding them in your mind and heart, repeat three times silently or aloud
May you be happy
May you be at peace
May you be safe
May you feel loved

Bring to mind someone towards whom you feel neutral. Holding them in your mind and heart, repeat three times silently or aloud
May you be happy
May you be at peace
May you be safe
May you feel loved

Bring to mind someone whom you find very challenging. Holding them in your mind and heart, repeat three times silently or aloud
May you be happy
May you be at peace
May you be safe
May you feel loved

Lastly, offering this blessing back to yourself, repeat three times silently or aloud
May I be happy
May I be at peace
May I be safe
May I feel loved

If going from negative thoughts and self-doubt to positive thoughts and self-love seems like too big a leap, aim first for a neutral approach. Strengthen your ability to think dialectically and find the gray area - shift away from good and bad, and tap in to a middle way of thinking. Practice taking a non-judgmental point-of-view.

For example, if negative self-talk is focused on your body image, consider first how you can find neutral. This comes with appreciating all that your body CAN do, like making it possible to share a hug or enjoy traveling. Find gratitude for your body.

This is also where Radical Acceptance comes into play. You don't have to like or agree with a situation, you don't have to judge it or label it, and you have to accept the reality of the situation.

What judgements do you hold about yourself?

Would you judge a friend similarly or have the same expectations?

How can you restate those thoughts to be non-judgmental?

Making Comparisons

Avoid the pitfall of comparing to others and remember to only compare to past versions of yourself.
Comparing to others leads to feeling inadequate, while comparing to other versions of ourselves can lead to insight.

It's easy to fall into the trap of comparing ourselves to others when most of what we see is a highlight reel, especially on social media. Remind yourself that social media and what people choose to disclose is never the whole story. We never truly know what is going on in the life of another human. As individuals we are each so unique that comparing to each other is a futile effort, because we are comparing to inevitably impossible standards.

Instead of comparing yourself to others, try instead comparing yourself to yourself. This introspective approach will give you a more accurate picture of how much you have grown and changed. Don't worry about what other people are doing, focus on you.

> Take a quiet moment to reflect on how you feel lately, and how this compares to other times in your life.

Identify a time when you felt worse that you do currently. What factors impacted you negatively?

Identify a time when you felt better than you do presently. What where you doing differently that you can bring back into your life?

Waning Crescent
Embracing the Shadow

To truly heal, we have to look at the stuff that makes us very uncomfortable. We all have a shadow side, otherwise we can't know lightness. The shadow holds the dark aspects of ourselves we have hidden due to shame, guilt, or negative experiences. Embracing the shadow is the work of the waning crescent, getting deeply reflective and unpacking the pieces of us hidden in dark corners.

Shadow Work

In "A Little Book on the Human Shadow," Robert Bly writes that we all carry around a bag with the aspects of ourselves of which we are ashamed.
He says: "When a woman puts her masculinity in a bag, or rolls it up and puts it in a can, she loses energy with it. So we can think of our personal bag (shadow) as containing energy now unavailable to us. If we identify ourselves as not being creative, it means we took our creativity and put it in the bag."

Unpacking the bag means sitting with the discomfort of the aspects of ourselves - parts that we have pushed away - and embracing them as valid and valuable. In order to sit with the discomfort, tolerate distress and stay emotionally regulated, we must be well resourced.

When reflecting and doing shadow work, it is extremely beneficial to be actively in therapy, processing and exploring adaptive ways of coping well.

Anything that we repress drains our energy. We have to be able to accept all the parts of ourselves to truly heal. Who would you be if you welcomed back the vulnerable, tender parts of yourself and got curious about them?

For example, after performing in local musicals throughout childhood, I found myself at college with much more serious competition. After a couple failed attempts at auditions, I put the performer part of myself in the bag. The part that loved singing and creativity went dormant and became shameful about enjoying the spotlight. Black and white thinking showed up as "I failed, so we're done here." This repressed shadow further manifested in less-than-helpful attention-seeking ways. Exploring that shadow part means bringing song, music, creativity and "the spotlight" into my life in ways that work more adaptively for me.

What have you put in your bag?

Grief

Everyone will encounter grief in their lifetime. Inevitably we will all experience deep loss. Understanding the process of grief is helpful in navigating what can be a very painful human experience.

Grief comes in stages. Understanding this process can help us allocate resources of support. According to Elizabeth Kubler-Ross in her 1969 book "On Death and Dying" the stages of grief include:

Denial -
"I can't believe it"
"This shouldn't have happened"

Bargaining - "If only I had..."

Anger -
Anger often shrouds other feelings. Look beneath the surface for another emotion that may be presenting as anger.

Depression -
The understandable sadness that accompanies loss.

Acceptance -
Eventually arriving at a resolution, acceptance brings less suffering and more peace.

Grief can show up in several aspects of life beyond loss of a loved one. The end of a relationship of any type, the end of a career, the end of a phase of life, loss of a pet, or any change can bring up grief. The stages of grief may be experienced as a non-linear process, revisiting each stage as needed.

Grief has no time limit as these emotions resurface with seasons, holidays, and reminders that show up in our lives.

Grief is a time of great reflection. Create space for yourself to grow around loss by journaling, creating, and finding ways to honor what was lost.

Super Moon
Super Charged Spiritual Practices

According to Farmer's Almanac, a Super Moon is when the full or new moon is closest to Earth such that it amplifies the gravitational pull causing higher tides. The Moon appears huge in the night sky as if you could reach up and touch her just above the trees. Four times a year, the Moon graces us with this magical show, and we gasp in awe at these moments of majestic beauty.

Spiritual Practices

Spiritual practices are beneficial to mental health and aid resilience. Ideally, a spiritual practice involves shared rituals and community support. They can take infinite forms with a common thread of connection to something greater. Mental health magic happens when we find tools that help us show up from a place of authenticity.

The act of intentionally clearing one's space both physically and energetically is a beneficial way to give yourself a reset.

Clearing, cleaning, and cleansing: Energetically clear your home, office or anywhere you spend time regularly. When mental health wanes, it can be difficult to find the motivation to care for our surroundings. The external environment is a reflection of the internal state. This may involve a morning or evening routine of straightening up daily.

Using sage, Palo Santo, incense, moon water spray, sage spray, sweeping, or any other practice will clear the energy of the space prior to spiritual practice. Light candles, burn incense, use an oil diffuser, sweep with a special broom, drum or use other instruments, turn on music - add whatever creates the energy in the space that you need in that moment.

Please note that smudging is a practice sacred to indigenous people. If this is not part of your culture, you are simply using smoke to cleanse the tools by visualizing that the smoke carry away any negative energy. Investigate and try cleansing practices sacred to your ancestors. I like to make moon water by charging water in the full moonlight with a few drops of essential oil and crystals in or on top of the jar.

Clear the energy of your space as often as you feel appropriate. Don't forget to cleanse yourself as well. If you are a helper, healer, or caregiver, you may want to do this more often.

Talisman and amulets: Consider how you adorn yourself - our jewelry can have powerful connections and offer protection. Find pieces you can wear that connect you to your spiritual beliefs, loved ones, ancestors, or simply feeling calm. Be sure to cleanse your jewelry, especially if it has been handed down through family or purchased as an antique. Jewelry holds energy, so make sure it's supportive.

What jewels or protective symbols can you draw upon for ancestral connection?

What can you wear that connects you to spiritual practices or something greater?

Vision Boards

Vision boards are a visual reminder of your goals and ways that you stay connected with your most authentic self. Making an annual vision board is one of my favorite manifestation practices. It keeps me inspired all year long.

A piece of poster board
Several magazines
A glue stick
Any glitter, stickers, markers, or craft supplies that make you happy!

1) Set your sacred space. Perhaps get yourself a cup of tea, put on music and light a candle. Do whatever sets the mood to connect with your intuition.

2) Enjoy perusing your magazine selection. Cut out any words or images that resonate with you. Don't overthink it. Some things that end up on your vision board won't make sense until several months from now.

3) Arrange and glue your vision board in a way that speaks to you.

4) Post your vision board somewhere you will see it daily as a reminder of what you are cultivating in your life.

5) Check back in with your vision board every month or so and notice what new meanings you can attribute or where something from the board has come into existence.

Crystal Practices

Crystals are one of my favorite magical coping tools. I wear them for their protective and healing qualities. When I look at different ones, I remember to cultivate those qualities within myself. Interacting with them reminds me of the magic and beauty that exists in nature.

To take a deeper look at which crystals are helpful for mental health conditions and learn more about crystal use and care, check out "Crystals for Emotional Healing" by Stacey Harrell.

Here are a few suggestions for an emotional support starter kit with meanings adapted from this book:

Amethyst: A crystal to support all types of healing, especially trauma, amethyst promotes calm and relieves stress and anxiety.

Labradorite: This stone supports self-worth and transformation, releasing lingering insecurity and fear.

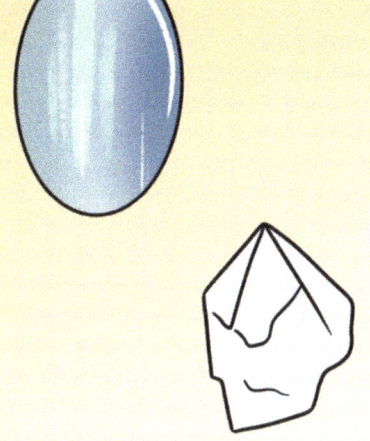

Moonstone: Strengthening intuition and connection to divine feminine energy, moonstone supports going with the flow, cultivating patience and calm.

Quartz: This crystal helps refocus and clear away emotional barriers and promotes perseverance.

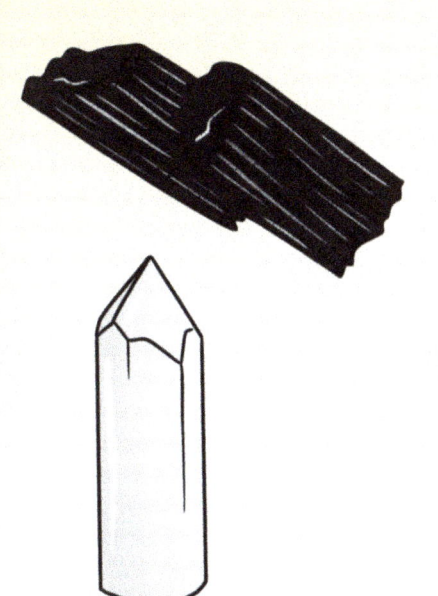

Black Tourmaline: This crystal is protective from negative energy and environmental stressors. Give over any negative thoughts and unhealthy habits to this guardian crystal.

Selenite: Queen of the clearing stones, selenite brings calm and tranquility, helping us stabilize and refocus. It's said to be helpful for insomnia.

Rose Quartz: The quintessential stone of love and trust in oneself, this stone attracts love and friendship and is supportive in times of grief.

In general, the color of the crystal and its healing qualities are correlated to the chakra system, an energetic system drawn from yoga. It outlines seven energy centers that travel up the spine from the tailbone to the crown of the head. Emotional and health related issues can be conceptualized through the lens of the chakra system. Crystals of similar colors are said to be healing to their respective energy centers. Dark crystals absorb negative energy, while clear crystals promote clarity.

Crystal Meditation

As a tool for coping with anxiety, crystals can be very helpful to ground through the senses.

Pick an interesting crystal with texture, sparkles, colors or an iridescent flash. I love using moonstone and labradorite for this activity.

Take a seat that feels respectful in your body. Close your eyes or find a soft gaze with eyes open (especially if you tend to check out when meditating or have trauma history).

Breathe.

Relax your face and shoulders and feel your seat in the chair.
Feel the crystal in your hands. Learn as much about the crystal as you can through your fingertips and sense of touch.

Breathe.

When you feel complete with touch, allow your gaze to move to the crystal. Relax your eyes, especially behind your eyes. Soften your cheeks and your jaw. Gaze at the crystal and learn everything you can about it through your sense of sight.

Breathe.

Continue until you feel grounded and centered.

Find a recording of this meditation by scanning the QR Code

Tarot and Oracle Cards

Cards have been used as a divination tool and means of guidance and connection to spirit for hundreds of years across many cultures. The symbolism and archetypes depicted in the cards' artwork and stories give the reader a means for introspection. The card reading is a container to project her thoughts and feelings. Tarot and oracle cards can serve as inspiration for self-reflective journaling.

Tarot cards are based on a specific system of seventy-eight cards which tell the same story of the hero's journey. Oracle cards are not structured and are based on creative inspiration. The possibilities are endless. Have fun finding artwork and authors who resonate with you and your interests.

A simple activity is to pull one card, investigate it, journal your thoughts, and look up the meaning in the guidebook.

I've offered a few more card layouts, also called spreads, on the following pages. You don't need to memorize anything to read cards. Sit with the images and notice whatever resonates with you. Reflect on how they relate to the questions posed in the spread.

Take this creative inspiration to your journal.

FOUR-CARD SPREAD

This is a simple reading for guidance. It can be applied to a specific situation or as an overview of a day or a week.

Overview: What is the overall theme of the situation?

Challenge: Who or what will cause conflict?

Outcome: What is the result?

Advice: How can I best support a successful outcome?

SHADOW WORK SPREAD

This reading is meant to prompt journaling about the shadow self and support unpacking the parts of ourselves of which we are ashamed.

EMOTIONAL BALANCE SPREAD

This reading offers a look at emotions and their impact. Consider an emotionally charged situation and let this spread guide you to journal.

5 — What do I need to feel grounded and centered?

4 — How can I validate my emotions?

1 — What is my current emotional state?

2 — What do I need to learn from my feelings?

3 — How can I authentically express myself?

CYCLE OF CHANGE SPREAD

This reading is meant to provide clarity around transitions and coping with barriers to change.

1) Pre-contemplation: What am I denying that needs to change?

2) Contemplation: What is getting in the way of making change?

3) Preparation: What can I do to address the problem?

4) Action: Who/What can support me through the discomfort of change?

5) Maintenance: What will help make this change sustainable?

6) Relapse: What challenges will arise when I change?

7) Center card: What am I meant to learn from this cycle?

Part 3

Coloring Pages and Creative Prompts

After all that education and information, it's a good time to take a brain break. Explore the coloring pages in this section as a form of creativity and mindfulness. As you're coloring, pay attention to the sensory experience of what colors you choose, how firm or light you're coloring, and the sound and feel of your tools on paper. Everytime you find your mind wandering away, pause and bring yourself back to the present and return to color mindfully.

Alternatively, use a page for a break during the day, or as a way of practicing completing a task piece by piece. Maybe you want to grab your coloring, a glass of lemonade, and head outside to a sunny spot for a brief mental vacation.

My Mental Health Apothecary

Fill up the bottles and jars below with a list of your internal and external resources, coping skills, and any other contents of your mental health toolbox.

Refresh your boundaries

As you color this Goddess' flowing hair, note in the sections what brings you joy.

Draw your Emotions

Draw your current emotional state in the frame below. When you're done, notice how you feel - both emotionally and physically - when you look at different parts of the picture.

Draw each emotion separately in the smaller frames below. Notice how you feel when you look at each picture.

Use these two pages to create a timeline of your life. Refer back to the shadow work activity and plot points at which you know you put something in the bag. Circle back to the phases of the goddess pages and mark where you transitioned into different phases. Consider all the significant events throughout your life and give them a home on this timeline.

Once you've completed the timeline, zoom out and look at the big picture of your life up to this point. What patterns do you notice? Where can you connect the dots? Reflect on this timeline, bring it to therapy, journal your reflections, or share it with a dear one if you feel so inclined.

Write a kind, compassionate, love letter to yourself from your Wise Mind Self.

Dump out whatever is swirling around in your mind right here.

Once you're done, take a moment to reread and reflect on your writing.
Respond to your brain dump here.

Your mind is beautiful, you belong here.

Hey Anxious Goddess,

Go forth and apply this deep study of yourself to show up authentically. The world needs your uniqueness.

Scan here to stay connected.

Acknowledgements:

This workbook would not exist without the support of very special humans for whom I am deeply grateful: my husband for supporting my entrepreneurial spirit and wild ideas; my parents for their unwavering encouragement of creativity; Kelly Rose Burgess for her creative vision and talent; Aaliyah Hamilton for creating the structure to begin this project; Kristen Indhal for her editing and discernment; and Jennifer Tuma-Young for her guidance on getting the best version of this workbook out into the world. Many thanks to all the teachers and colleagues who've shared their healing wisdom throughout the years- especially Dr. Joanne Jodry, Dr. Phyllis Alongi, and Jillian Pransky. The most enormous gratitude to all the clients I've had the honor of supporting - thank YOU for trusting me to be a companion on your mental health journey.

About the Author

Jamie Hanley is a Licensed Professional Counselor who practices through a holistic and intersectional feminist lens. Having experienced how much yoga helped her manage anxiety, Jamie integrates yoga therapy techniques such as mindfulness, breath work, meditation, and guided relaxation with cognitive interventions when supporting clients. She encourages clients to honor their biological cycles and lean into cyclical living.

Throughout her career, Jamie has taught hundreds of clients how to prioritize their mental health needs, learn coping skills, and live in alignment with their values. In her free time, she finds joy in snuggling with her family and kitties, crafting, reading, and gardening. She believes in everyday magic and synchronicity, is known to wish on angel numbers, pull oracle cards for guidance, and throw salt over her shoulder for good luck.

Learn more about her at jamiehanley.com and on instagram @jamiehanley_

About the Illustrator

Kelly Rose Burgess is an artist and illustrator, with degrees in both Culinary Arts and Graphic Arts. Kelly has been creating The Goddess Collection for almost a decade, with her Goddesses inspired by women who are unafraid to wield their power and celebrate their strength, while letting their inner beauty shine through. Kelly's multimedia artwork has been featured in local art galleries and exhibits.

Most recently, Kelly has been creating more "self-care" types of art pieces to connect with her own mental health journey of coping with anxiety and panic attacks.

Kelly lives joyfully with her husband and dogs in New England.

For more information please visit her website, bananalovemuffin.com or find her online @bananalovemuffin.

Mental Health Organizations

NAMI: National Alliance on Mental Illness
nami.org
Helpline 1-800-950-NAMI (6264)
text "HelpLine" to 62640
or email us at helpline@nami.org

Teen & Young Adult Helpline
1-800-950-6264
chat, text "Friend" to 62640
or email helpline@nami.org

MHA: Mental Health America
mhanational.org/get-help

www.ingramcontent.com/pod-product-compliance
Lightning Source LLC
Chambersburg PA
CBHW041314240426
43669CB00024B/2979